308.
43
BAL

Women in early modern England, 1500–1700

D1426184

072150

introductions to history

Series Editor: David Birmingham,
Professor of Modern History, University of Kent at Canterbury

A series initiated by members of the School of History at the
University of Kent at Canterbury

Published titles

David Birmingham
The decolonization of Africa

Christine Bolt
*Feminist ferment: "The woman question" in the USA and England,
1870–1940*

G. M. Ditchfield
The Evangelical Revival

Jacqueline Eales
Women in early modern England

Doreen Rosman
*From Catholic to Protestant:
religion and the people in Tudor England*

Kevin Ruane
War and revolution in Vietnam, 1930–75

Bruce Webster
The Wars of the Roses

Forthcoming titles

David Birmingham
The Atlantic Empires, 1400–1600

S-M. Grant
The American Civil War

Oonagh Walsh
Ireland's independence

David Welch
Hitler

Women in early modern England, 1500–1700

Jacqueline Eales
Canterbury Christ Church College

LEARNING CENTRE

CLASS
NO: 305.43 EAL

ACC
NO: HW 025227

072150

WOMEN

SOCIOLOGY

WOMEN

HARROW COLLEGE
HH Learning Centre
Lowlands Road, Harrow
Middx HA1 3AQ
020 8909 6520

© Jacqueline Eales 1998

This book is copyright under the Berne Convention.
No reproduction without permission.
All rights reserved.

First published in 1998 by UCL Press

UCL Press Limited
1 Gunpowder Square
London EC4A 3DE
UK

and

1900 Frost Road, Suite 101
Bristol
Pennsylvania 19007-1598
USA

The name of University College London (UCL) is a registered
trade mark used by UCL Press with the consent of the owner.

British Library Cataloguing in Publication Data
A catalogue record for this book is available from the British Library.

ISBN: 1-85728-268-X

Typeset in Sabon and Gill Sans by
Acorn Bookwork, Salisbury, UK.
Printed and bound by T.J. International, Padstow, UK.

Contents

	Abbreviations	vi
	Preface	vii
1.	Women, gender and patriarchy	1
2.	Historiography and debate	7
3.	Historical sources	16
4.	The nature of women	23
5.	Literacy and education	35
6.	Politics	47
7.	The family	60
8.	Work	73
9.	Religion	86
10.	Crime and the courts	98
	Conclusion	110
	Bibliography	113
	Index	127

Abbreviations

BL British Library
CCA Canterbury Cathedral Archives
EBD *The Europa biographical dictionary of British women,* A. Crawford, T. Hayter, A. Hughes, F. Prochaska, P. Stafford and E. Vallance, eds (London: Europa, 1983)
HMC *Historical Manuscripts Commission, fourteenth report; Appendix, part II: the manuscripts of His Grace the Duke of Portland,* vol. 3 (London: Eyre and Spottiswoode, 1894)
PRO Public Record Office
SP State Papers
SR *Statutes of the realm* (London, 1810–28), vol. 4

Preface

This book is an introduction to recent historical writing about women in early modern England. Over the past two decades or so there has been a vast increase in research into the lives of women in all past ages and we owe the resulting expansion of our knowledge primarily to two distinct intellectual developments. The first of these is the role played by feminist theorists in prompting historians to investigate crucial questions about the fashioning of women's roles and rights in past societies. The second is the impact of social history, whose exponents have shunned the traditional focus of political historians on battles, dates, kings, queens and parliaments in favour of what might be termed 'people's history'.

This emphasis on history from the bottom up inevitably embraces all sections of society – men, women and children alike – and also serves to remind students of women's history that the influences of class, race, religion and the family were as important as issues of gender in past societies. The fertile cross-influence of the disciplines of gender studies and social history has also led historians to reconsider the role of women in specific political or religious developments. In the early modern period this includes the Reformation, the nature of court politics in the Tudor and Stuart period, the English Civil Wars and the religious and political aftermath of the Restoration. New findings which take the involvement of women into account in these and other areas are signposted throughout this book.

Within the brief format presented here it is, however, impossible to consider fully every aspect of the now burgeoning research and debate about early modern women. The primary purpose of this text therefore is to stimulate the initial interest of both students and general readers. In particular the bibliography is intended to help those who wish to investigate individual topics in greater depth.

Many intellectual and personal debts have been incurred in the course of writing this book and I would like to thank Tony Claydon, Penelope Corfield, Grayson Ditchfield, Fiona and Richard Gameson, Stephen Hipkin, Lynne Hulse, Shonaidh Marsh, Tim Wales, Diane Willen and Sonia Wynne for their advice on specific points, and Graham Durkin, Amy Erickson and Sally Minogue for kindly commenting on earlier drafts. Richard Eales has provided moral support as well as the critical medievalist's perspective essential to prevent early modernists from constantly reinventing the wheel. Finally my thanks to Kevin Ruane for his good humoured interest in this project, to the editors at UCL Press, Steven Gerrard and Aisling Ryan, for their support and encouragement and to Gerard Hill for efficient copy-editing.

For Lindsay, Moira and Vivienne

CHAPTER ONE

Women, gender and patriarchy

In 1624 Sir Edward Conway greeted the birth of his grandson, Edward Harley, with joy both for the safe delivery of the mother and, as he pointedly observed, the 'advantage of the sex' of her child (*HMC*). Conway's words encapsulate the nature of relationships between men and women in early modern England. The sex of the child at birth was biologically determined, but thereafter the specific benefits accorded to him as a male were the products of the society and culture into which he had been born. To Conway these social advantages seemed as natural as the physical distinctions between the two sexes: the one flowed from the other.

Young Edward Harley was doubly privileged: as a first-born male member of the social elite he could look forward to an education at university, a public career as a local magistrate and member of Parliament, and the inheritance of the bulk of his father's estates. In contrast, his four younger sisters, Brilliana, Dorothy, Margaret and Elizabeth, were barred as women from studying at the two English universities of Oxford or Cambridge, they could not take high public office and, although they could expect to receive dowries, by virtue of primogeniture only a relatively small proportion of their father's wealth would be transferred to them. By custom, rather than law, they would not vote for their brother in parliamentary elections and, if they married, their legal identities would be absorbed by that of their husbands. Under common law a married woman – a feme covert – could not contract or sue independently of her husband.

Edward Harley's life merits an entry in the *Dictionary of national biography*, but none of his sisters is separately noticed there. It is important to remember, however, that the privileges accorded to him were class-based. Most men could not vote because they did not fulfil

1

the requirements of land ownership for county elections or of membership of a town oligarchy for the boroughs. Only a minority of men received the academic education offered by the grammar schools and the universities, and most men could not aspire to the highest political and legal posts.

This book is concerned in the main with the years 1500 to 1700. These dates are not rigidly observed since neither social nor women's history lends itself to exact periodization in the way that political events do (Wiesner 1998). Nevertheless, for over a quarter of the period under consideration the throne was occupied by queens – Mary I (1553–8), Elizabeth I (1558–1603) and Mary II (1688–94). Queen Anne's reign, from 1702 to 1714, lies just outside the scope of this survey, but early eighteenth century material has been considered where relevant. Mary I's reign marked the first involvement of a woman in politics at the highest level since the unsuccessful efforts of Matilda to gain the crown in the mid-twelfth century. The brevity of Mary's rule and her failure to secure the future of Catholicism in England contrasted strongly with the success of Elizabeth in establishing a Protestant religious settlement and in maintaining stability in England over four and a half decades.

After her death Elizabeth's reign came to be seen as a 'golden age' of peace and prosperity. The unprecedented example of successful female monarchy did not, however, lead directly to any radical changes in the lives of ordinary women. Like the first female British Prime Minister, Margaret Thatcher, the Tudor and later the Stuart queens were more concerned with establishing their primacy over male subordinates than in addressing any questions of inequality between the sexes. One distinctive feature of the early modern period that allows us to monitor whether a trickle down effect in favour of women was in operation or not was the expansion of print culture. Works about the nature of women were published throughout the period to satisfy the demands of an increasingly literate readership. The literature demonstrates that traditional views about the inferiority of women continued to dominate the market, and works calling for change were in the minority.

The sixteenth and seventeenth centuries also encompassed two key events in the development of the modern British state – the Reformation and the English Civil Wars. These events had a considerable long-term impact on the lives of ordinary people and both have been seen as important catalysts of change for women in particular. The spread of

Protestantism in England from the early 1520s onwards encouraged women to take part in religious debates, and the spread of non-conformist religious sects in the 1640s and 1650s had a similar influence. The Reformation also encouraged literacy amongst the laity and, it has been suggested more contentiously, helped to elevate the status of women within both the home and society more generally. Similarly, during the 1640s and 1650s many women took over the responsibilities of men who were at Westminster, in exile, or involved in the fighting in England, Wales, Scotland and Ireland. Whether the Reformation and the Civil Wars did indeed result in long term gains for women is a matter of debate and these questions will be analyzed more thoroughly in the following chapters of this book.

Any investigation into the lives and experiences of women in the past must take account of how earlier societies have defined the relationship between the sexes. In the early modern period women were described by male authors as morally, intellectually and physically weaker than men. This analysis was based primarily on biblical teaching and on contemporary medical understanding. The story of Adam and Eve and the New Testament writings of St Paul were influential sources of religious arguments for the subordination of women. They were reinforced by Aristotle's theory that a woman was physically an inferior version of the perfect male form and by the traditional belief that there was a balance of the four humours in the human body. According to humoral medicine, men were believed to be hot and dry and women were cold and moist, making them passive, intellectually unstable and lacking in courage.

In the sixteenth century the most advanced medical thinking developed in France, Italy and Germany, where the growth in anatomical knowledge meant that in professional circles there was a marked shift away from belief in the humoral system by 1600. In the long term this contributed to a change in attitudes towards women, but these ideas were slow to penetrate England and the most popular anatomical work in early Stuart England, Helkiah Crooke's *Microcosmographia* (1615) was still heavily influenced by humoral beliefs. It was not until the late seventeenth century that Thomas Gibson's *The anatomy of human bodies epitomised* (1682) and William Cowper's *The anatomy of human bodies* (1697) presented more accurate anatomical findings to a wider English audience, but popular thinking followed more slowly. Although women were believed by most religious, medical, legal and moral theorists to be inferior to men, they were not seen as naturally submissive and therefore various restraints were imposed on women in order to reinforce the social order (Maclean 1980; Sommerville 1995).

The development of feminist thinking certainly played an important role in altering perceptions about women. From the mid-seventeenth century, women began to argue that the restraints imposed on them originated not from any innate inferiority of the female sex, but from society's understanding or construction of what was appropriate male and female behaviour, in other words from nurture rather than from nature. Modern feminist theorists have adopted the term gender to identify the distinctions between men and women which are socially constructed (Scott 1986; Lerner 1986; Riley 1988). Despite this definition the boundaries between differences of gender and of sex are often difficult to identify and are still open to debate (Corfield 1997).

As Sir Edward Conway's words cited at the beginning of this chapter indicate, social meanings are attributed to sex from the moment of birth. As a result the extent to which psychological or emotional differences between the sexes are innate or culturally determined is more difficult to assess than, for example, the historical origins of distinct dress codes for men and women in different societies. Yet, broadly speaking, within a feminist model of society the sexual distinctions between men and women can be said to be those which are biologically determined, while differences of gender can be defined as those that are culturally constructed.

Since the 1970s the influence of gender studies has provided women's history with greater theoretical clarity. The mapping of how definitions of male and female behaviour have changed over time has revealed the differences between men and women which were specific to past cultures, the ways in which they were reinforced and how they have changed over time and place. Women in early modern England were disadvantaged because they were born into an overtly patriarchal society. In its broadest sense patriarchy means the political and social dominance of men over women and children. In early modern England male dominance was reinforced through a fully articulated political theory of patriarchy in which the function of men as heads of households and as fathers was believed to be analogous to the role of the monarch. The family was regarded as the most important unit of social organization and it was seen as both the origin of civil society and as a microcosm of the state itself.

Political, religious and legal authorities thus drew a parallel between power in the state and that of the father within the family. Both forms of authority were natural and God-given and, just as the ruler or his officials represented the best interests of the subjects, the father was responsible for and represented the needs of his family. Disobedience to either political or paternal jurisdiction was seen as unnatural and, it was believed, would lead to widespread disorder. Such patriarchal theories were commonplace in sixteenth- and seventeenth-century England and were derived from a variety of earlier classical and medieval writers as well as from the Bible, which was regarded by contemporaries not only as a guide to religious and moral behaviour, but also as a social and political blueprint. Patriarchal theories did not go unchallenged, particularly by republican writers during the 1650s, and they found their most formidable opponent in John Locke, who argued for a separation of royal and fatherly power in *Two treatises of government* (1690). Locke and subsequent writers did not, however, abandon the notion that fathers were the natural heads of households (Schochet 1975; Amussen 1985, 1988; Ezell 1987).

There was also a gulf between theory, which for much of this period was exclusively composed by male authors, and practice, which involved negotiation between men and women on a daily personal basis. Many of the most influential authors of the time were clerics and, because women could not share in their ministerial functions, they drew very rigid lines between the public duties of men and the household responsibilities of women. In practice, the boundaries between the private and public spheres were diffuse and this was reinforced by the personal nature of political and other forms of patronage as well as by economic structures (Eales 1998). Furthermore, differences of class could also cut across the gender divide. Very few theorists maintained that all women were inferior to all men and aristocratic or gentry women expected and received deference from men and women who were not their social equals.

The extent and influence of patriarchal control has therefore been the subject of considerable debate and two distinct and influential master narratives about the status of women in early modern English society have emerged. The older of these is a story of progress, which argued that the educational and spiritual standing of women was elevated in England in the sixteenth and seventeenth centuries by the effects of both the Renaissance and the Reformation. This interpretation was based on humanist demands for better female education coupled with the Protestant emphasis on the important role to be played by women in promoting godliness in the home amongst children and servants. The more recent interpretation is a story of decline, which posited that the growth of capitalism and the Industrial Revolution had a damaging effect on the economic status of women. This analysis was founded on the belief that for much of the early modern period the production of goods and foodstuffs was largely centred on the home where women could exercise some measure of control. By 1700 the growth of larger scale production, the accumulation of capital and the growth of the wage economy were beginning to erode the economic independence of women.

Both of these narratives have been challenged by detailed research dating from the late 1970s onwards and the next two chapters will survey some of the most important contributions to these debates. Chapter Three will consider what contemporary sources can be used to investigate these issues further. Ensuing chapters will look at early modern theories about women, as set out primarily by male writers, and compare these with social practice in the realms of politics, the family, work, religion, and crime and the courts.

CHAPTER TWO

Historiography and debate

In 1973 Sheila Rowbotham published an important study of women in Britain from the sixteenth century to the 1930s. Her account was written from a feminist perspective and was entitled *Hidden from history: 300 years of women's oppression and the fight against it.* Implicit in her title was the belief that the experiences of women had been largely missing from previous historical accounts. Since the publication of Rowbotham's book, interest in and research into women's history have expanded dramatically. In part this is a response to the modern feminist movement dating from the 1960s, but writing about women of past ages has a considerably longer pedigree. Historical writing about women has always been influenced by more general historiographical trends and until the early twentieth century this was reflected in the dominance of the biography as the main form of historical inquiry into the lives of women. This was partly the result of the pre-twentieth century preoccupation with the influence of the famous individual on the course of world history, but it was also based on a tradition of eulogizing virtuous individuals, both men and women, as role models.

The praise of good women can be traced back into the classical world in the biographies written by Plutarch and the saints' lives of the early Church. It was continued into the middle ages by the *Golden legend*, written by Jacobus de Voragine in the mid-thirteenth century, which contained the lives of both male and female saints and continued to be one of the most popular books until the Reformation. Secular works also helped to develop the genre in the later middle ages, most notably Boccaccio's *Concerning famous women*, Christine de Pisan's *Book of the city of ladies* and Chaucer's *The legend of good women*, in which Chaucer included Cleopatra as well as mythical figures such as Queen Dido (Davis 1976). The English dramatist, Thomas Heywood, was writing in this tradition when he published his *Gynaikeion: nine books of various history, only concerning women* (1624). His subjects were drawn largely from classical history or mythology such as the goddesses Juno and Minerva, the muse Clio, the Amazons and Sybils, and learned women such as Hypatia and Sappho. He also incorporated biblical characters such as Rebecca and Esther as well as more recent historical figures. Heywood contrasted the noble behaviour of these famous women with the ignoble behaviour of others, and one section of his book concerned incestuous and adulterous women and those who suffered 'strange' deaths. The work ended with a moralising section on the punishments of the vicious and the rewards of the virtuous.

Heywood followed this with an account of the *Exemplary lives and memorable acts of nine [of] the most worthy women of the world* (1640), which provided a pantheon of heroines to match the traditional nine male worthies. His subjects were a mixture of biblical, mythical and historical figures and were grouped together as three Jews (Deborah, Judith, Esther), three pagans (Penthisilaea, Artemisia, Boadicea) and three christians (Ethelfleda, Margaret of Anjou and Elizabeth I). Heywood did not interpret their heroic exploits as typical of womankind. He regarded them as extraordinary women whose achievements were largely the result of their 'masculine spirited' characters. This was the line also taken by Elizabeth I's earlier biographer, William Camden, who wrote that 'by these manly cares and counsels, she surpassed her sex' (Haigh 1988).

As the discipline of history became more professional the use of mythical individuals as exemplars of admirable male and female behaviour gave way to a more rigorous analysis of the lives of individuals. This approach had its origins in the practice of preaching funeral sermons which included a short biographical sketch of the departed. The preachers of these works drew on stereotypes of godliness, but the sermons also had to be personalized and they often contained biographical information supplied by family members or friends that cannot now be obtained elsewhere. Funeral sermons were printed in increasing numbers from the late sixteenth century and by the second half of the seventeenth century the biographical elements were separately printed as cycles of godly lives. Samuel Clarke, the dissenting minister, was instrumental in this development and his last work, *The lives of sundry eminent persons in this later age* (1683) contained biographies of twenty-five clerics and gentlemen, and nine women, including his own wife Katherine and the countesses of Warwick and Suffolk (Eales 1990b). Clarke was working within a religious tradition and saw himself as a successor to John Foxe, whose *Acts and monuments*, relating the stories of the Marian martyrs, had first appeared in English in 1563.

A more secular mood was reflected in the collections of biographies of notable women written by George Ballard in 1752 and by Mary Hays, the first woman to make a notable contribution to the genre, in 1803. An intellectual watershed was reached in the mid-nineteenth century with the publication of Agnes and Elizabeth Strickland's *Lives of the queens of England* (1840–48) which surveyed the lives of forty queens from Matilda, wife of William the Conqueror, to Queen Victoria. The Stricklands worked from a variety of original sources including medieval chronicles, state papers and private archives, and were influenced by the need for objectivity in the writing of history emphasized by academic historians such as the German Professor Leopold von Ranke. 'Facts, not opinions', should be the motto of every 'candid historian', noted Agnes Strickland, although the work was coloured by the belief that as women the queens of England were a civilizing force: 'our great object being to present ... the history of female royalty, to trace the progress of civilization, learning and refinement in this country, and to shew how greatly these were affected by queenly influence in all ages'.

The first serious attempt to investigate the lives of early modern women as a social group, rather than through the study of worthy individuals, was made by Alice Clark in her *Working life of women in the seventeenth century* (Clark 1919). Clark was an active campaigner for women's suffrage and her research was conducted after she took up a studentship at the London School of Economics in 1913 at the age of thirty-eight. Clark's work was strongly influenced by the feminist and socialist thinking of the day and she argued that the seventeenth century represented 'an important crisis in the historic development of Englishwomen' as economic production was separated from the household. Women were consequently forced into more limited domestic roles and their capacity as wage earners fell as they were unable to compete with skilled male workers. This process could first be discerned in the seventeenth century and was compounded by the later effects of the Industrial Revolution.

Clark's analysis was widely accepted until the 1980s when case

9

studies of women in individual regions or specific occupations began to challenge some of her basic assumptions. These studies have revealed that there was not a progressive, linear decline in the economic importance of women, but rather that there was considerable variation in the experiences of different groups of workers and social classes. Female work patterns fluctuated according to local conditions, and during times of expansion women might be encouraged into certain areas of production or trade only to be edged out in favour of male workers in times of decline. The differentiation between wages paid to men and to women was already apparent in the late middle ages and was not, as Clark thought, a characteristic of the changes taking place in the seventeenth century. Moreover, changes in the organization of the market economy increased the independence and wage-earning capacity of women in some occupations (Charles and Duffin 1985; Prior 1985; Underdown 1985; Cahn 1987; Vickery 1993).

At the same time that Clark's work was coming under critical scrutiny an older interpretation of the historical forces that had affected women in the early modern period was also in the process of being revised. The belief that Protestantism had introduced new and more positive attitudes towards women, marriage and sexuality has had a lengthy history. The medieval Catholic Church's insistence on clerical chastity meant that anti-female arguments had been widely employed by the pre-Reformation clergy to reinforce the merits of celibacy as spiritually superior to marriage. In contrast, the reformed clergy – many of whom, like Luther and Calvin, were married – insisted that they held marriage and wives in greater esteem than did their celibate Catholic opponents. This assessment of their own writings dominated all subsequent historical analysis about the social impact of the reformers in England until the mid-1960s and it was widely accepted that the Reformation had generated a new theory of domestic relations in which the role of women was elevated. Historians drew evidence from printed Elizabethan and early Stuart conduct books and sermons to argue that Protestant teaching placed increased importance on love, companionship and shared responsibilities between husbands and wives in the ordering of their families. This emphasis was believed to be most strongly expressed by the puritans, the more radical wing of the Protestant Church in England (Haller & Haller 1942; Schücking 1969).

These assumptions were first challenged by Christopher Hill in *Society and puritanism* (Hill 1964) when he anticipated later feminist scholarship by arguing that, although the Reformation had reduced the authority of the priest in society and replaced it with that of the father in the family, this did not improve the position of women. Hill described the theology of Protestantism as patriarchal, 'reducing the role of the Virgin and of the saints, many of whom were women'. This opinion was largely supported by Lawrence Stone in his influential work on *The family, sex and marriage in England, 1500–1800* (Stone 1977) where he argued that early modern Protestant preachers and moral theologians were zealous in advocating the total subordination of wives and that a trend towards greater patriarchal control in husband–wife relations was developing in the sixteenth century. Paradoxically, however, this was accompanied in practice by growing evidence of affection within families.

The divergence observed by Stone between theory and practice is important and has also been highlighted for different reasons by Kathleen Davies, who has suggested that the ideal family of the conduct books did not exist even among puritan families. Davies pointed out that Church court records and popular customs indicate that, amongst the poor, attitudes towards marriage and family life 'remained unchanged over many centuries' and since the conduct books were theoretical guides they were no real indication of how men and women actually behaved. She also argued that the advice given to the laity on domestic issues in pre-Reformation works was very similar to that given by later puritan authors and that there was no distinct Protestant theory of domestic relations.

Her arguments have been supported by Margo Todd, who has demonstrated that sixteenth-century christian humanists, such as Erasmus and Vives, anticipated the precepts of the Protestant reformers, and by Ian Maclean, who has found that there was less change in attitudes towards women during the Renaissance than the 'intellectual ferment and empirical enquiry' of the period would lead one to expect. Maclean grounds the restrictions placed on women in the sixteenth and seventeenth centuries on the christian institution of marriage, which restricted any fundamental reassessment of the role of women in society. This issue has been addressed more recently by Margaret Sommerville, who argues that there were few issues on which the English Protestant writers diverged significantly from either their medieval Catholic predecessors or their Catholic contemporaries. She concludes that much of puritan teaching on women and the family was 'utterly conventional' and that puritan preachers 'generally just

11

repeated ancient platitudes' (Davies 1977, 1981; Todd 1980; Maclean 1980; Sommerville 1995).

This growing consensus has been challenged by Anthony Fletcher, who suggests that the 'fashionable view' that English Protestant writers had little new to say should be reconsidered. His reading of their works is influenced by modern feminist reinterpretations of St Paul's New Testament writing. Thus Fletcher highlights the value placed in the puritan conduct books on the physical aspects of marriage, which cut across the Augustinian objection to sexual pleasure, seeing it instead as a positive preservative against adultery. He interprets this approach to sexual relations within marriage as a 'radical departure' from previous teaching. In a major survey of gender relations between 1500 and 1800 Fletcher has further argued that attitudes towards women changed in the period not only as a result of medical progress but also because of the development of the more secularized mechanical philosophies of the seventeenth century. Men's attitudes towards women thus moved from a misogynistic and negative fear of their potentially disorderly sexuality to a more positive construction of womanhood as chaste, desexualized and domesticated, amongst the elite classes at any rate (Fletcher 1994, 1995b). Fletcher locates the origins of this positive view of women in the early modern period, but it does have a longer history and can be traced back to the Church Fathers. It was strongly expressed in the medieval Catholic literature on the lives of female saints, which had played an important part in constructing a positive image of feminine religious observance and motherhood via the models of St Anne and the Virgin Mary well before the Reformation.

The re-evaluation of the extent to which Protestantism affected the status of women has been mirrored by a similar debate about the effect of Renaissance and humanist ideals on their education. In the early sixteenth century, humanist scholars such as Erasmus, Thomas More and Vives promoted the benefits of a classical education for boys in order to prepare them for public office. They also wrote in favour of educating women, although their learning was to be put to domestic uses where it would enable them to be obedient to their husbands and to raise their children religiously. As a result of these theories a number of prominent Englishwomen did acquire humanist and classical learning; and the scholarly achievements of More's own daughter Margaret, of Mary and Elizabeth Tudor, Lady Jane Grey and her sisters, and the daughters of Sir Anthony Cooke, amongst others, have often been cited as evidence of the positive impact of the new learning on the general education of women in the period (Gardiner 1929).

More recently, however, considerable doubts have been raised about the wider impact of these developments and Ruth Kelso was amongst the first to argue that renaissance writers had very limited aims for the education of women and were in fact tentative in their treatment of the subject. Joan Kelly has famously queried whether women had a Renaissance at all and has argued that the humanist stress on female passivity and chastity further contributed to the subordination of women. Hilda Smith has also pointed out that the learned women of the Tudor court numbered no more than fifteen high-profile individuals and, although new educational opportunities were opening for men, these remained closed to women. Moreover, after the death of Elizabeth I a reaction against learned women was apparent at the Stuart court (Kelso 1956; Kelly 1977; Smith 1982).

Current historical thinking thus suggests that attitudes towards female inferiority were not greatly altered by either the Reformation or the Renaissance. Indeed the early Protestant reformers placed greater responsibility on the heads of households for the religious behaviour of their dependants, thus reinforcing patriarchal control within the family (Maclean 1980; Roper 1989). Humanist education produced a new caste of male secular administrators, but it also pushed women further into the ranks of the disadvantaged in comparison with the opportunities available to elite males (McMullen 1977; Friedman 1985). In the economic sphere attempts by women to exploit opportunities for greater independence resulted in an apparent backlash that amounted to what David Underdown has described as a 'crisis in gender relations' in the period 1560–1660. The crisis was characterized by an intensification of prosecutions against women as scolds and witches, and by an increase in popular public demonstrations, charivari, against domineering wives (Underdown 1985). Although Underdown's argument has been influential it is based largely on evidence drawn from the towns and parishes of Wiltshire, and more detailed local research in other counties needs to be undertaken to test its general validity for the period as a whole.

The debates outlined above suggest that the social and economic status of women was not the subject of progressive improvement from the late middle ages to the modern period. The Protestant reformers did little to elevate the position of women, humanist education was restricted to a minority at the highest levels of society, and women were unable to compete economically with men. 'Radical' or 'revolutionary' feminists would go even further in arguing that the sixteenth and seventeenth centuries constituted a period of continuous oppression of women by men characterized by the witchcraft trials of the period (Hester 1992). The latter conclusion has not, however, found general acceptance amongst historians and it runs counter to recent research that stresses the active agency of early modern women in many different capacities.

There were areas where women could legitimately exercise authority through the social status of their family and their own role in their communities. They were, therefore, able to promote the rights of their family or to protect communal privileges in the same way that men did. A clear example of this is the ability of women to inherit property in the failure of male heirs. In the mid-sixteenth century the accessions of Mary and Elizabeth Tudor and of Mary Stuart, as queen of Scotland from 1542 until her forced abdication in 1567, were seen as part of this legitimate operation of inheritance. There is little evidence that any of these queens was opposed purely because of her sex, apart from the publication in 1558 of the notorious diatribe against the government of women by the Scottish Protestant exile John Knox, *The first blast of the trumpet against the monstrous regiment of women*, which was directed at both Mary Tudor and Mary Stuart. Knox's position was atypical and he was actively refuted by a number of English and Scottish writers (Shephard 1994).

Similarly, a number of aristocratic women inherited titles or property in their own right. More generally some twenty per cent of all marriages produced only daughters and their right to inherit from their parents was generally acknowledged. Women could also intervene in court and local politics in order to protect their family interests. In an era when the political process rested on both dynasticism and patronage, the involvement of women was accepted. In 1646 Dr William Denton informed the exiled Sir Ralph Verney that 'women were never so useful as now' in pleading with the parliamentarian committees for the security of their estates since 'their sex entitles them to many privileges' (Erickson 1993; Slater 1984). Throughout the period elite women were also involved in obtaining offices, grants or favours from the monarch and the exercise of influence over local officials. Women participated in the maintenance of networks of political and social patronage through the bestowal or exchange of gifts such as food or jewellery (Harris 1990; Bowden 1993). They owned patronage rights such as the advowson of clerical livings, which allowed them to appoint the next incumbent, and there are even rare examples of women exercising the right to nominate members of Parliament in rotten boroughs. Women were also actively involved in marriage negotiations on behalf of younger relatives which would help to extend the power of their own family.

The exercise of political influence largely concerned the landed elites, but women lower down the social scale could also represent their families in various ways. Women were invariably participants in food riots during times of dearth and high prices for they were regarded as knowing what the morally acceptable price should be, as well as having the right to protect their families and the community from the extortionate costs of basic foods. Women also acted as arbiters of neighbourly behaviour in their communities and they made use of informal sanctions as well as the machinery of the Church courts to discipline those who overstepped the sexual or moral line. The religious divisions of the Reformation also provided an area where women could become involved in endorsing what they believed was the true faith on behalf of family and community. The spiritual authority of individual religious charismatics had been recognized by the Catholic Church before the Reformation, but Protestantism also gave women of all social classes the opportunity to become involved in religious debates and many of the Marian martyrs were women of humble social backgrounds (Walter 1980; Gowing 1996; Crawford 1993). Women of all ranks had a variety of ways, therefore, in which they could have some measure of social authority.

One consistent factor which emerges from the various debates and secondary works outlined above is the almost universal agreement amongst historians that there was a divergence between the ideal behaviour of men and women, outlined by prescriptive writers, and actual social practice. In terms of interpretation much depends therefore on the types of sources used by historians to investigate the past and the next chapter will examine the available sources for women's history in greater detail.

CHAPTER THREE

Historical sources

The most obvious source material for the historical study of women's lives is anything written by women themselves and especially printed works, which would have been accessible to a wider contemporary audience than private manuscripts and thus might have played a part in shaping public opinion. The immediate problem is that English-women wrote very few printed books before the middle of the seventeenth century. Until 1600 most women whose works did go into print – such as Lady Margaret Beaufort, Margaret Roper, Lady Ann Bacon, or Mary Sidney, the Countess of Pembroke – did so as translators of works written by men, although in some cases they did extend and develop the original text. Notable exceptions to this include Anne Askew's highly personal account of her interrogation prior to her execution as a Protestant heretic in 1546, and the uniquely combative *Jane Anger her protection for women* of 1589.

This last purported to be a defence of women against the detractions of men, and it has been widely accepted as the first printed contribution by a woman to the literary debate about the nature of women, the so-called *querelle des femmes*. Yet nothing is known of the author and her name suggests a humorous *nom de plume* that could have been adopted by a man. It is the earliest of a small group of pamphlets written between 1589 and 1640 which have been uncritically accepted as early examples of feminist writing by women (Kelly 1982; Ferguson 1985; Henderson & McManus 1985). Three of these works were printed in 1617 in reply to Joseph Swetnam's *The arraignment of lewd, idle, froward, and unconstant women* (1615) – an attack on the character of disorderly women, which also contained a 'commendation' of 'wise, virtuous and honest' women. The replies in defence of women were Rachel Speght's *A mouzell for Melastomus*,

Esther Sowernam's *Ester hath hang'd Haman* and Constantia Munda's *The worming of a mad dog.*

As with Jane Anger, nothing is known about the authors except for Rachel Speght, who has been identified as the daughter of a clergyman. A further pamphlet appeared in 1640 – in response to the work of John Taylor – under the pseudonyms of Mary Tattle-well and Joan Hit-him-home, *Women's sharp revenge.* Despite the female personae adopted in these five texts there is no certainty that any of them were in fact penned by a woman, except that by Rachel Speght. It has been suggested that Taylor himself wrote *Women's sharp revenge* and if this were the case he certainly would not have been the first male author to write on both sides of the debate about the nature of women in order to publicize and sell his work (Shepherd 1985).

It has been argued, however, that even if these pamphlets were written by men they can still be described as feminist (Henderson & McManus 1985). This is misguided, since a feminist analysis depends upon the argument that the subordination of women is based on ideology, whereas these pamphlets repeat the traditional arguments that female inferiority was based on nature or divine command. Thus Jane Anger berated men for taking advantage of 'the weakness of our wits and our honest bashfulness'; Rachel Speght noted that Satan first assailed Eve because 'she being the weaker vessel was with more facility to be seduced'; Esther Sowernam argued that a wife was commanded to obey her husband in order to increase her own glory, for 'nothing is more acceptable before God than to obey' (Shepherd 1985). These and other defences of women are not early feminist statements since they do not claim equality between men and women, nor do they define an agenda for equitable change. Moreover, their content is double-edged, for in order to defend women their authors have to repeat the calumnies made against them. These pamphlets thus reproduce some of the same misogynistic material contained in the literary attacks on women by Swetnam and others, and their interpretation is by no means straightforward.

Women began to publish their own clearly identifiable original works in growing numbers from the beginning of the seventeenth century. Patricia Crawford has identified forty-two first editions written by women and published between 1601 and 1640, and these books mainly addressed religious or domestic concerns. The decade 1641–1650 represented a turning-point, when 112 new editions by women were printed, more than all the new works published by women before 1641. The gap in numbers between male authors and female authors is striking and Crawford has calculated that between 1600 and 1640 women's publications accounted for only half of one per cent of all published material. The proportion rose between 1640 and 1700 to a mere 1.2 per cent.

The coincidence of this increase with the social dislocation caused by the Civil Wars and the execution of Charles I is significant, for the early 1640s witnessed the collapse of the government censorship system which had previously controlled the contents of published books. From 1640 there was a marked increase in books on current affairs, and women joined in the general religious and political debates that were generated by the disputes between King and Parliament. After the Restoration, works of poetry, drama and fiction were produced by Aphra Behn, the first Englishwoman to earn a living exclusively from writing, and works on female education and marriage by Mary Astell. Women also contributed to the new scientific enquiries that became fashionable in the reign of Charles II; and Margaret Cavendish, Duchess of Newcastle, wrote a variety of literary and philosophical books (Crawford 1985; Hobby 1988; Hunter & Hutton 1997).

The sparse number of books produced by women before the mid-seventeenth century also provides us with indirect evidence of the low level of female literacy in England, which according to David Cressy may have been as little as one per cent in 1500 and never rose above thirty per cent before 1700 (Cressy 1980). These figures are based on the ability to form a signature, but there are problems in using this as an indicator of literacy, because it is difficult to gauge the extent of an individual's skills from a simple signature. Cressy's figures may be indicative of the numbers of women who could read and write, but not of those who could only read, which is more difficult to assess. A low female literacy rate makes the use of women's private papers problematical. Handwritten letters, diaries, commonplace books, religious reflections, memoirs, and medical or other household recipes do survive from the period, but were primarily written by aristocrats and gentlewomen, who were amongst the most likely to be fully literate and whose families were given to amassing archival collections in their country houses. Their lives and opinions were undoubtedly very different from those of agricultural or textile workers, servants, the poor, or women living in urban centres (Mendelson 1985).

Some of the private papers of the period have been published in scholarly modern editions and these include the earliest surviving diary kept by an Englishwoman, the puritan Lady Margaret Hoby, written in the years 1599–1605, and the autobiography of Lady Grace Mildmay (1552–1620), both of which reveal a preoccupation with religious and domestic concerns. In contrast, the memoirs written by Lucy Hutchinson, Lady Anne Fanshaw and Lady Ann Halkett, all of whom lived through the Civil War years, also provide evidence about the deepening political crisis of the time (Meads 1930; Pollock 1993; Sutherland 1973; Loftis 1979). These memoirs can be compared with the letters of Lady Brilliana Harley, written mainly in the period 1638–1643, which show the gradual disintegration of traditional social ties in her home county of Herefordshire at the outbreak of civil war in 1642 and how her strong puritan convictions strengthened her resolve to support Parliament against the king (Lewis 1854; Eales 1990a). Historians are now also uncovering the important role that women played in the development of practical medical knowledge, and in the scientific and philosophical advances of the period. The medical papers of Lady Grace Mildmay show that like many other women of her rank she prepared her own medicines, but she produced them on a large scale for use outside her home (Pollock 1993). Such personal manuscripts survive in increasing numbers throughout the period, which is partly indicative of increasing literacy rates amongst women in general, but also reflects greater care taken with family papers amongst the elite classes.

Institutional records can provide evidence for larger numbers of individuals lower down the social scale. Wills, and the associated documents of probate inventories and accounts, can supply historians with a great deal of evidence about property-owning, kinship networks and, on occasion, religious inclination. The problem here is that generally only the wealthier members of society made wills. Probate inventories are more likely to have survived for those lower down the social scale, but were only required if the estate was worth more than £5. Furthermore, these documents would not necessarily list all of the property owned by an individual. Wills did not specify gifts that were made before death while inventories concerned moveable goods only and thus did not necessarily list land, although leases might be mentioned.

Such problems are compounded in the case of women, since a married woman was unlikely to draw up a will, since her husband retained any property that was not subject to a marriage contract or trust. Wills made by women accounted for 400,000 or 20 per cent of all wills made between the mid-sixteenth century and the mid-eighteenth century. Nearly 80 per cent of these were made by widows, nearly 20 per cent by single women and less than 1 per cent by wives. Amy Erickson has pointed out that although women made wills less often than men, nevertheless women were usually named as executrices in their husbands' wills. This involved women appearing before the Church courts to prove wills, exhibit inventories of the deceased's moveable goods and to file probate accounts a year after the death. These activities provide some of the best examples of women's financial responsibilities and management in the period. Using probate documents and records of lawsuits over marriage settlements, Erickson has charted the pattern of property ownership by women in the early modern period.

The property rights of women were circumscribed by common law, which dictated that in general wives could not make wills without their husbands' permission and that widows were entitled to a life interest in only a third of their husbands' real property. These conditions could be modified by equity, manorial law, church law and statute law, and as a result women enjoyed substantial property interests of their own, although these were under threat by the late seventeenth century. Before that date there is evidence that below the ranks of the landed elite daughters and sons inherited equitably from their parents. Girls usually received personal property and their brothers received real property, although when there were no sons then daughters usually inherited any land and this may have been the case in roughly 20 per cent of marriages. Wives made settlements that protected the property they had brought to their marriages, and widows were entrusted with more property and financial responsibility than was required by law. Yet the period also saw the progressive domination of common law doctrines and this resulted in a deterioration of the legal rights of women as property owners by 1800 (Lansberry 1984; Erickson 1993).

Records of ecclesiastical lawsuits are a valuable source of information, not only about property but about a range of other issues. The Church courts dealt largely with people in the middle ranks of society rather than the elite or the very poor. Where depositions from such witnesses have survived they can help to reconstruct the attitudes of men and women below the social elites. The ecclesiastical authorities could prosecute men and women for failing to conform to the religious orthodoxy of the day, perhaps by not attending church regularly or by using the wrong service book. Such cases furnish evidence of the early spread of Protestant belief, of resistance to the Reformation by Catholic recusants, or of the growing influence of radical puritan beliefs before the Civil Wars.

Church courts could also prosecute for sexual transgressions such as pre-marital intercourse (which might be described as incontinence, fornication or whoredom) and adultery. These types of cases provide evidence of sexual activity which contravened the prescriptions of the conduct literature and also show that women were more likely than men to be presented for sexual immorality. The Church courts also heard cases between the laity and these could include disputes over wills, breach of promise over marriage, and defamation. This last category gradually came to dominate such party-versus-party cases, and women played an increasing role as plaintiffs in Church court cases designed to defend their reputations against slander (Sharpe 1980; Gowing 1996). The ecclesiastical courts ceased to function during the Civil Wars and there are considerable gaps in their records during the 1640s and 1650s.

The records of secular courts are also being exploited by historians to investigate the type of crime associated with women, who were more likely than men to be prosecuted for scolding, infanticide and witchcraft. The records show that a significant minority of women were accused of theft, normally of household goods of relatively little value. The study of crime in all periods is complicated, however, by the fact that not all criminal acts are reported; and in the early modern period research is affected by the uneven survival of court records. A great amount is known for example about witchcraft prosecutions in the county of Essex, where the records of the most important local criminal courts, the quarter sessions and the assizes, are very full (Macfarlane 1970). For the county of Herefordshire, however, very few records for these courts have survived before the Restoration. Such disparities make it impossible to state with complete accuracy how many prosecutions or executions for witchcraft, or indeed any other crime, took place in England as a whole.

This chapter has been concerned so far with published works, personal papers, wills and court cases, all of which are sources that can reveal women's own articulation of their experiences and expectations. There are other more quantifiable sources – such as parish registers, poor law records, tax and census lists – that can be used to recreate information about the population as a whole, information about such things as demographic movement, wealth and family formation. Women can sometimes be under-represented in such documents and such source-related problems will be discussed later. Before examining what the historical evidence reveals about the lives of women between 1500 and 1700, the next chapter will consider the attitudes towards women that were contained in the prescriptive literature of the age.

CHAPTER FOUR

The nature of women

In the early modern period the vast majority of books were written by men and they analyzed the nature of women in a variety of different published genres. The writers of works which prescribed the ideal behaviour of women were heavily influenced by classical, biblical and medieval arguments, and they cited the story of Adam and Eve as well as authorities such as Aristotle, St Jerome, St Augustine, and Thomas Aquinas in support of the widely held belief that women were the inferior sex (Sommerville 1995). The traditional estates literature of the middle ages had analyzed men's roles in society according to their estate or social rank, but when medieval and early modern theorists considered women they generally divided them into virgins, wives and widows thus placing a central emphasis on the importance of marriage to their status.

Religious, political and legal writers concluded that the differences between the sexes were divinely sanctioned, natural and designed to fit women for running the household and men for public duties. They wrote for what they regarded as an exclusively heterosexual audience. Male homosexuality was regarded as both a crime and a sin, while female homosexuality was treated as an intriguing, but not entirely serious subject (Bray 1995). Medical and sensationalist writers addressed the problems of hermaphrodites, but most other authorities restricted their comments to the heterosexual population.

Two competing views of the characteristics of women were developed. On the one hand women who ignored the precepts of religion or lacked the guidance of an effective male relative were potentially a source of disorder and sexual licence. They were typified as shrews, wantons and even witches. On the other hand women who internalized religious prescriptions and were obedient to the male head of their household were seen as role models for duty and piety, whether they were mythical or historical figures, saints or ordinary women. These two contrasting views of womanhood were common themes not only in the prescriptive literature of the day but also in fiction, ballads, drama, poetry and other forms of popular entertainment (de Bruyn 1979).

Following the political destabilization of the English Civil Wars in the mid-seventeenth century, a small number of female writers began to challenge these traditional assumptions. Margaret Cavendish, Duchess of Newcastle, and Mary Astell have been described as amongst the first English feminists because their works not only display an awareness of the social construction of gender, but are also a critique of its failings from a feminine point of view (Smith 1982). They argued that the inferiority of their sex was not innate and was perpetuated by a lack of education. They believed that, given the same intellectual training, women would be as rational and as capable of exercising political or intellectual judgement as men. Yet their influence was isolated and it might be better to term these writers proto-feminists, for no wider women's or feminist movement grew up until the mid-nineteenth century when the sustained demand for female suffrage prompted the organization of pressure groups with a programme for change.

Before 1700 the belief that women had to be kept in check by male authority was almost universally accepted and was reinforced by the teachings of the Church both before and after the Reformation. The Protestant marriage service in *The book of common prayer* of 1559 exhorted women to heed the teachings of St Paul and 'submit yourselves unto your own husbands, as unto the Lord, for the husband is the wives head, even as Christ is the head of the Church'. These prescriptions were amplified in the Elizabethan *Homilies* first published in 1563 and ordered to be read at church services when there was no sermon.

The *Homily of the state of matrimony* stated that marriage was ordained by God so that men and women should live in perpetual friendship, have children and avoid fornication. The homily quoted St Peter in advising husbands to treat their wives as 'the weaker vessel'. Wives were to command their children and family, but not their husbands, whom they should obey as Sarah uncomplainingly obeyed Abraham. A good part of the homily was taken up with arguing that both parties should be patient with the other. The husband was warned not to beat his wife under any circumstances, even if she was 'a wrathful woman, a drunkard, and beastly, without wit and reason' for anger and dissent would hinder prayer, which was essential to bring the couple closer to God and create harmony between them.

In the early modern period one of the most influential bodies of prescriptive literature was contained in conduct books which set out the respective duties of husbands and wives. They sold in their greatest numbers between the late sixteenth century and the Civil Wars and they are a valuable source of information about gender construction. Kathleen Davies has suggested that these books were popular because they reflected the ideals of what she calls the 'urban bourgeoisie' (Davies 1981). Most of the authors of conduct books were clergymen and – despite Davies' assertion – they did not regard the laity as ideal role models for marriage. The Protestant clergy were keen to defend and define marriage because this was a boundary by which they distinguished themselves from the Catholic ministry, and the model of clerical marriage was more important to them than has previously been recognized (Eales 1998).

The biblical precepts quoted in the marriage service and in the *Homily* were expanded in the advice books and sermons of popular clerical authors such as Thomas Becon, John Dod, Robert Cleaver, Henry Smith, William Whately, William Gouge, Thomas Gataker, Thomas Taylor and Richard Baxter. They all followed the teachings of St Peter and St Paul in stressing the subjection of wives to husbands and this was reinforced by reference to the Fall of Mankind. William Gouge argued in *Of domestical duties* (1622) that 'good reason it is that she who first drew man into sin, should now be subject to him, lest by the like womanish weakness she fall again'. Gouge emphasized that the wife was 'joint governor with her husband' over their children and servants, but she was subordinate to her husband and ruled others only as long as she was obedient to him.

At the start of *A bride-bush: or, a direction for married persons* (1619), which was based on a marriage sermon, William Whately described a woman's 'chiefest ornament' as 'lowliness of mind, which should cause her to maintain ... a mean account of herself, and of her own abilities'. At one point he even warned that a woman who believed herself to be her husband's equal or his superior could not attain a state of grace, or spiritual salvation. Whately realized that a wife might be her husband's social superior, but even then she was required to show wifely submission.

25

Like St Paul, Whately also placed great importance on women remaining silent in front of their husbands and other men, for 'at all times, amongst all wise folk, the talkativeness of women before men (chiefly their husbands, and most of all when it comes to loud and earnest speaking) hath gone in the reckoning of a fault, and a sign of self-conceitedness and indiscretion' (Eales 1998). Fear of women's tongues was a consistent theme in prescriptive literature. Thomas Becon wrote in his *New catechism* (1561) that nothing 'doth so much commend, advance, set forth, adorn, deck, trim and garnish a maid as silence'. Over a century later the royalist cleric Richard Allestree referred in *The ladies calling* (1673) to 'this great indecency of loquacity in women' and their 'mere chatting, prattling humour, which maintains itself at the cost of their neighbours'. Allestree was one of the most influential prescriptive writers of the late seventeenth century. His book continued to be reprinted into the early eighteenth century and had a considerable influence on the growing courtesy literature of the turn of the century (Fletcher 1995b).

Margo Todd has argued that women were regarded as 'only slightly inferior' to men by both the humanists and later Protestant authorities, but it is hard to agree with this conclusion (Todd 1980). Gouge wrote that husband and wife were not equal and that 'the extent of wives subjection doth stretch itself very far ... even to all things' and Whately stated that the wife was not her husband's equal 'yea, that her husband is her better by far'. Richard Baxter explained the position of women in *A christian directory* (1673) as being 'betwixt a man and a child: some few have more of the man, and many have more of the child, but most are but in the middle state'.

In what ways then was Protestant teaching on marriage and women innovatory? Along with denying that marriage was a sacrament, English and continental reformers also rejected both the Catholic belief that celibacy was a more honourable state than marriage and the theological tradition that held that all sexual activity, even within marriage, was potentially sinful and corrupting. It was not that the English clergy were introducing novel ideas about marriage – indeed in some respects, notably the subject of divorce, they were remarkably conservative – but importantly they were adapting traditional views to fit their own situation as married men (Eales 1998).

For Davies, however, the advice given by Protestant writers was only innovative in two respects: first, that there was no merit in voluntary sexual abstinence by married couples and, second, in the suggestion that divorce and remarriage were permissible for the innocent party in cases of desertion or adultery. This last point was in line with continental reformed theory and practice; but, as Ingram has pointed out, these more radical measures had not been adopted in England, where it was only possible to obtain a separation on the grounds of adultery or cruel behaviour and the marriage remained undissolved. William Whately was one of the few clerical writers to argue in favour of more permissive divorce and in this he anticipated the arguments of John Milton and John Selden put forward in the 1640s. It was not until 1670 that Lord Roos established the right to divorce by private act of Parliament, a solution that was used only twice before 1700 (Davies 1981; Ingram 1987; Durston 1989; Phillips 1991).

What was also certainly new was the example of the clergy extolling the virtues of marriage from personal experience, and Anthony Fletcher has described the enthusiasm and openness with which they discussed sexual pleasure within marriage as a radical new departure (Fletcher 1994). The legality of clerical marriage was first recognized in Edward VI's reign and it led to the creation of clergy families with traditions and expectations of their own. In defining marriage the Protestant clergy drew on traditional concepts of social and gender order that would enhance their own authority as legitimate heads of patriarchal households.

When advising their parishioners about the ideals of marriage, it was not the example of lay marriage which they offered as a model; it was their own version of domestic order and of gender roles that they proposed as the ideal. It depended for its greatest success on husbands and wives who had internalized the precepts of early modern gender construction better than most and they were to be found amongst the clergy and the young women whom they had trained within their own households. The ideal family – in which wives, children and servants were benignly ruled by a wise, patient, God-fearing patriarch – found its fullest expression in the homes of the clergy, where the God-given authority of the father was doubly reinforced both as father and as minister. A number of the authors of conduct books were married to clerics' daughters including John Dod, whose first wife was a stepdaughter of Richard Greenham, William Whately, whose wife Martha was the daughter of George Hunt, and Thomas Gataker, whose second wife (of four) was the daughter of the reverend Charles Pinner.

Girls who were raised in clerical housholds were given an exceptional training and as a result they were highly susceptible to the conventional teaching about patriarchal authority. After the Reformation they were quite often taught to read and write, but their reading material was restricted to religious and improving works. Elizabeth Joceline, whose work *The mother's legacie* of 1624 is widely cited as evidence of female religiosity and humility, was raised in the home of her maternal grandfather, the Bishop of Chester, where she was taught languages (including Latin), history and 'some arts', but principally studies of piety.

As an orphan Elizabeth Calton, later the wife of William Gouge, boarded at the house of an Essex minister, John Huckle of Hatfield Broad Oak, 'whose wife had a great name, and that not without just desert, for skill and faithful care in training up young gentlewomen'. When Elizabeth Gouge died in 1626 she was characterized as 'a pious, prudent, provident, painful, careful, faithful, helpful, grave, modest, sober, tender, loving wife, mother, mistress, [and] neighbour'. Valentine Overton, the rector of Bedworth in Warwick trained his daughter Katherine to write out the sermons she heard and repeat them, as well as to learn William Perkins' *Catechism* by heart. When she died at the age of 73 in 1675, her husband the puritan minister Samuel Clarke wrote that 'as a wife she was singular, and very exemplary in that reverence and obedience, which she yielded to her husband, both in words and deeds. She never rose from the table, even when they were alone, but she made courtesy, she never drank to him without bowing. His word was a law unto her: she often denied herself to gratify him' (Eales 1998, 1990b).

The boundaries of gender construction may well have been negotiable for gentry wives with dowries and large estates to administer in their husbands' absences, or for city wives, such as Gouge's parishioners at Blackfriars in London, who took him to task for saying that women could not dispose of the common goods of the family without or against their husband's consent. For the wives of the clergy such negotiation was more limited. There were no formal opportunities for a cleric's wife to share in his ministerial functions, and unlike many other wives, she could not continue his work if she were widowed. This point has previously been overlooked by historians, but it explains why clerical conduct book writers put such great stress on the division between the public duties of the husband and the private domestic duties of the wife. Within lay families the boundary between the private and public domains was considerably more diffuse.

Another important source of prescriptive writing about women was contained in 'godly' biographies and funeral sermons, which were printed in increasing numbers from the 1580s onwards for the aristocracy, the gentry, the clergy, and their wives. One of the earliest and most popular biographies of a godly woman was the gentleman Philip Stubbes' *A christal glass for christian women* (1591) extolling the brief life of his wife Katherine, who had died at the age of nineteen after four years of marriage. Katherine was depicted as giving over her entire life to religious reading and observance and 'when she was not reading she would spend her time in conferring, talking and reasoning with her husband of the word of God and of religion'. So popular was *A christal glass* that it was reprinted over twenty times between 1591 and 1640.

Funeral sermons usually contained a brief biography of the deceased, which was obviously idealized to a certain extent, but which also had to be recognizable to the family and friends in the congregation. These sources invariably described their female subjects as pious, charitable and reticent, but often also as meek, gentle and tenderhearted. They stressed the importance of wives' maternal role and their subjection to husbands and other male relatives. Individual women were described as practical examples of how to fulfil the biblical injunctions to obey their husbands. On marrying, Lady Alice Lucy, who died in 1648, resigned both her 'reason and her will unto her head, her husband', while Lady Elizabeth Langham, who died in 1664, made frequent use of St Paul's injunction contained in 1 Corinthians 14: 35, for 'when she desired to learn anything' she asked her husband, from whom she would receive instruction 'in all submissive silence or quietness' (Eales 1990b).

The few female authors of James I's reign had largely accepted these doctrines. Dorothy Leigh stated in *The mother's blessing* (1616), written for her children, that she wanted her book to encourage women to 'give men the first and chief place ... let us labour to come in the second, and because we must needs confess that sin entered by us into our posterity, let us show how careful we are to seek to Christ to cast it out of us and our posterity'. In *The mother's legacy* (1624) written for her unborn child, Elizabeth Joceline wrote 'if thou beest a daughter, remember thou art a maid, and such ought your modesty to be, that thou shouldst scarce speak, but when thou answerest'.

The stress placed on female silence and respect for husbands recommended in conduct books and sermons does not of course mean that this was universally put into practice. Their authors were also worried about what they saw as the prevalent lack of respect, as well as the domestic and wider disorders that would ensue from it. The *Homily of the state of matrimony* feared that there were few marriages without 'chidings, brawlings, tauntings, repentings, bitter cursings and fightings' and blamed this on the popular belief that men should command their wives with 'fist and staff' and also to the common habit of women in scolding their husbands, calling them 'fools, dastards and cowards'.

William Whately thought that some women had 'inverted the Apostle's precept, causing their husband to stand in fear of them'. Such behaviour, he warned, would lead to the 'harlot's house', for a woman who would cast off her loyalty to her husband would soon abandon her sexual honesty. He added disapprovingly that 'we have some women that can chase and scold with their husbands, and rail upon them, and revile them'. Whately was at odds with the majority of English clerical opinion of the time when he argued in *A bride-bush* that a husband could use blows as a corrective, if his wife had repeatedly and wilfully disobeyed him and refused to comply with reasonable commands.

The clear implication of these texts is that women needed the restraints imposed upon them by religious teaching and by the authority of their husbands, because without them they would be untrustworthy, overtalkative and weaker in judgement than men, and the more easily tempted by lust and pride into sin and disorderliness. Such a view of womankind was consonant with theological teaching about the Fall and the sinfulness of Man, but it should be remembered that men were also seen as potential sinners. Typical male vices included drunkenness, gluttony and physical aggression.

Negative constructions of femininity found much more extreme expression, however, in the medieval and early modern literary debate about women now known as the *querelle des femmes* (Kelly 1982). The participants in the debate tended to generalize from the particular, so examples of individual women were taken to represent the virtues or vices of their sex as a whole, according to the argument being put forward. Thus the Roman matron Lucretia, who committed suicide after suffering rape, was frequently cited by defenders of women to illustrate female chastity and sexual honour. Whereas

Xanthippe, the nagging wife of the Greek philosopher Socrates, was cited against women as evidence of their inclination to scold and undermine their husbands.

Early printed contributions to the *querelle* in England included the anonymous *The schoolhouse of women* (1541) which characterized women as lustful, chattering drones intent on cuckolding their husbands, whose reason was not 'worth a turd'; and Edward Gosynhill's *The praise of all women* (*c.* 1542), in which he catalogued examples of virtuous women from the Bible and from classical stories. Gosynhill has been suggested as the author of both of these works and if so they were intended to be contrasting pieces and not necessarily statements of his own thinking (Henderson & McManus 1985).

Similar problems of interpretation surround the translation of Heinrich Agrippa's *Treatise of the nobility of womankind* (1542), in which he praised women as men's superiors. It would be a mistake to herald this as an early feminist statement. It has been described as a 'rhetorical paradox' and the author himself admitted that in his defences of women he included many 'invalid arguments and jests' (Woodbridge 1984; Maclean 1980). The *Treatise* can thus be seen as defence of an indefensible proposition, an elaborate extended joke which would raise smiles amongst the educated men who read the original Latin version or its later English translation. It was certainly not intended as a serious rebuttal to the conventional attacks on women, which characterized them as sharp-tongued viragos, prone to the sins of lust and pride. Attacks on the characters of women continued to prove popular and Joseph Swetnam's *The arraignment of lewd, idle, froward, and unconstant women* went into ten editions between 1615 and 1637. In 1639 John Taylor published two works, *Divers crabtree lectures: expressing the several languages that shrews read to their husbands* and *A juniper lecture*, along similar lines.

The opinions against women voiced in the *querelle* were echoed in the more ephemeral popular literature of the day such as chapbooks and ballads, which portrayed women as potential sources of disorder. Margaret Spufford has noted that anti-feminine chapbooks invariably presented women as sexually insatiable, but also that this genre depicted romantic love and a wide range of sexual behaviour before marriage. These attitudes and practices were also reflected in the romantic fiction, poetry, plays and other entertainments of the age (Spufford 1981). Ballads similarly dealt with popular attitudes towards women and had such graphic titles as *A ballad which doth plainly unfold the grief and vexation that comes by a scold* (1588) or *Anything for a quiet life; or the married man's bondage to a curst wife* (*c.* 1620). Chapbooks and ballads reinforced patriarchal codes both by emphasizing the value of chastity and the virtues of a good wife, as well as by exposing the supposed weaknesses of women. A ballad entitled *The virgin's ABC or, an alphabet of vertuous admonitions for a chaste, modest and well-governed maid* (1656) thus advised young women not to laugh too much nor to offend with a foul and slandrous tongue. *A country new jig between Simon and Susan* (*c.* 1620) describes a loving relationship between a young couple intent on marriage, but also shows them seeking the approval of the girl's parents. Other ballads show the disastrous results of young women giving way to lust and being left on their own with an illegitimate child (Rollins 1922; Marsh 1995).

Similar themes were dealt with in the dramatic literature of the period. The medieval cycles of morality plays had, for example, drawn on Eve and the Virgin Mary as contrasting types of feminine behaviour. The traditional religious plays and pageants of the Catholic Church were suppressed by the reformers before the end of Elizabeth's reign. There was also a simultaneous drive against popular festivities such as May games and Christmas mis-rule, which parodied the social and sexual orders in order to emphasize the dangers of disorder, but which were associated in the minds of Protestants with pre-Reformation superstition. Lisa Jardine and Kate McLuskie have demonstrated that issues of sex and gender were also central motifs in the emerging drama of the late Elizabethan and Jacobean stage. More specifically plays such as Shakespeare's *The taming of the shrew* (1594) drew on the debate literature to dramatize contemporary concerns about the links between gender and social order (Jardine 1983; McLuskie 1989; Fletcher 1995a).

A developing critique of these traditional views can be found in the increasing number of works written by women from the early 1600s onwards, although female authors were relatively rare until the mid-seventeenth century. This development was partly a product of the breakdown of the censorship of printed books during the civil war period, which encouraged women to publish more freely. It was also a result of the growth of female literacy which drew authors from a range of social groups into the debates about women. The educationist Bathsua Makin was the daughter of John Pell, rector of Southwark; Judith Drake, the author of *An essay in the defence of the female sex*

(1696), was the daughter of a Cambridge solicitor; and the political philosopher Mary Astell, who was born in Newcastle upon Tyne in 1666, was descended from merchant families in the town.

One of the earliest original female authors was Elizabeth Cary, Viscountess Falkland, who was the first Englishwoman to write a tragedy, *The tragedy of Mariam* (1613), in which she explored the idea that women should be allowed to divorce their husbands. Hilda Smith has argued, however, that it is not until the mid-seventeenth century that the first arguably feminist publications appear in print. She has identified a number of influential seventeenth century proto-feminist writers including Bathsua Makin, Hannah Woolley, Margaret Fell and Mary Astell.

Amongst the earliest writers in this group was the royalist Margaret Cavendish, Duchess of Newcastle, who published fourteen works between 1653 and 1668, which included poetry, plays, philosophy, essays and letters. In *The worlds olio* (1653) the Duchess declared that the sexes were created equal but that men had 'usurped a supremacy to themselves' and had tyrannized women, using them like 'children, fools or subjects'. This process enslaved women and dejected their spirits to the point of stupidity, 'whereas in Nature we have as clear an understanding as men'. According to Smith the core of Cavendish's work, although intermittent and haphazard, was 'the issue of sexual distinction in structuring society'.

One of the most systematic of the writers identified by Smith was Mary Astell, whose works were designed to defend her conservative and High Church Tory political views against those of the more radical dissenting Whigs. Two of her books particularly concerned the role of women in society. The first of these was a *A serious proposal to the ladies*, printed in two parts in 1694 and 1697, in which she argued for the foundation of a female retreat or 'monastery' where women could study without taking any formal vows. Astell argued that the incapacity of women was 'acquired not natural' and that it stemmed from 'ignorance and a narrow education'. The second was *Reflections upon marriage*, published in 1700 in which she attacked the Whig belief in the right to resist tyranny by comparing political power to the balance of power within marriage. Astell deliberately attacked the work of John Locke when she wrote, 'if absolute sovereignty be not necessary in a state, how comes it to be so in a family?'. Her answer was not that women should be freer within marriage, but that 'she then that marries ought to lay it down for an indispensable maxim that

33

her husband must govern absolutely and entirely, and that she has nothing else to do but to please and obey' (Cerasano and Wynne-Davies 1996; Smith 1982; Hutton 1997; Hill 1986; Springborg 1996).

Astell and other women writers of the late seventeenth and early eighteenth centuries had not yet adopted a fully coherent feminist position. Their views on the role of women were largely at odds with the arguments of more mainstream male theorists, whose attitudes towards women, as Sommerville argues, remained largely unchanged between 1500 and 1700. The strictures on female behaviour set down in the prescriptive literature of the Protestant clergy demonstrate a tension in their works between the two competing views of women as either excessively pious or open to temptation and vice. Their fears about women's potential failings fed straight into the more overtly misogynistic literature of the *querelle des femmes* as well as the popular chapbook fiction and ballads of the day.

The role of print culture in disseminating these views is extremely important, because it made them widely available and both reflected and shaped cultural expectations about gender. Writers who developed proto-feminist theories about the nature of women, such as Margaret Cavendish and Mary Astell, were particularly concerned that a disparity of education created the gulf between the sexes. Theories about women's education, which concerned the upbringing of girls before marriage and the educational opportunities available to them, will be considered more fully in the next chapter.

CHAPTER FIVE

Literacy and education

The steady growth of literacy rates and the increased number of grammar schools in England in the sixteenth and seventeenth centuries have been described as part of an 'educational revolution' by Lawrence Stone. These changes were prompted by the growth in both government bureaucracy and commerce, and by the demand for greater professionalism amongst the clergy and the legal profession. The revolution was shaped by humanist and Renaissance ideas about learning, which advocated that boys should be fully prepared for their future roles both as administrators and citizens of the state (Stone 1964; O'Day 1982).

Humanist writers also advocated better educational provision for girls, but though this advice affected the education of women in court circles there is little evidence that it made much impact on the content of girls' education more widely. It has also been argued that even elite women were largely excluded from the new humanist learning and Linda Pollock notes that the upbringing of elite girls continued to be largely aimed at producing 'adult women who were deferential to men', but who were also capable of independent action if occasion arose. Nevertheless, there is wider evidence that women's literacy did increase in the period, although it remained lower than that of men. There was also considerable concern amongst moralists and educationalists about what types of books were suitable for women and some, such as Elizabeth Cary and Lucy Hutchinson, while encouraged to read by their fathers, encountered opposition from their mothers to their excessive bookishness (McMullen 1977; Friedman 1985; Pollock 1989; Pearson 1996).

Throughout the sixteenth and seventeenth centuries women had very restricted access to educational institutions and were barred from admittance to the two universities at Oxford and Cambridge or to the Inns of Court in London, where lawyers were trained. Although young girls as well as boys attended the petty or dame schools, where elementary reading and writing was taught, there was a great divergence in schooling and educational opportunities for the two sexes. Boys from the elite social classes could attend grammar schools, where they were prepared for the universities, but there is no hard evidence that girls ever did so in significant numbers. Those schools that catered especially for girls were intended to impart skills that were seen as useful for women, rather than classical learning.

The evidence does suggest, however, that more educational provision, both formal and informal, was becoming available to them. The number of women who could form a signature grew over the period and inventories reveal that women were increasingly owners of books. This was, of course linked to the growth in print culture at the time and in particular the expansion in the numbers of printed books aimed specifically at women from the 1580s. From the late sixteenth century there was also an increase in the number of boarding and other schools for girls, although the education they offered continued to be training for their future roles inside the family as wives, mothers and mistresses of households.

One of the most influential European writers on women's education in the sixteenth century was the Spanish humanist Juan Luis Vives, who produced a Latin treatise on the subject in 1523 under the patronage of Katherine of Aragon. It was translated into English in the late 1520s as *The instruction of a christian woman* and went into nine English editions by the end of the century. Vives linked chastity with learning, which would occupy the mind wholly, lifting it to a knowledge of goodness and raising it from things that were 'foul'. The mind would thus be able to resist unchaste thoughts. To this end Vives argued that girls should avoid the reading of romances and instead study the Bible, patristic writers such as Jerome, Cyprian, Augustine and Gregory, and classical authors such as Plato, Cicero and Seneca.

Unlike boys, who were taught the art of public speaking or rhetoric, Vives believed that a girl had no need of eloquence; instead 'she needeth goodness and wisdom'. Rhetorical skills were needed by boys if they went on to take a career in the law, or become clergymen, magistrates or members of Parliament. For humanists the ability to speak publicly was part of the education a man needed to fit him for his future role as an active citizen. The assumption in Vives' work, and that of other humanists, was that only exceptional women, such as Mary Tudor, would ever take such a public role. Vives also famously advised that women should not be allowed to teach, because 'woman is a frail thing and of weak discretion and . . . may lightly be deceived, which thing our first mother Eve sheweth, whom the Devil caught with a light argument'.

He expanded on the education of women in *The office and duties of a husband*, an advice book for husbands which appeared in an English version in the 1550s. Here he advised that women should not have trivial or superstitious books or meddle with 'curious and deep questions of divinity', but should read virtuous, holy books and works of moral philosophy. A knowledge of grammar, logic, history, politics and mathematics should be left to men. Vives also repeated his injunction against eloquence in women and advised the husband to number silence amongst his wife's virtues, 'the which is a great ornament of the whole feminine sex' (Watson 1912).

The educationist Richard Mulcaster expressed similar views in his *Positions* (1581) where he described giving young women any kind of learning as 'but an accessory by the way'. He suggested that girls should be educated because of the excellent effects that this would have and specifically they should be taught to read, as this was necessary to teach them about religion. For Mulcaster, as for most Elizabethan educators, the woman's role was to govern her house and family and to deal with sickness. He noted that girls' brains were not so much 'charged, neither with weight nor with multitude of matters, as boy's heads be' and that physically they were weaker from which he concluded they were intellectually less able.

Mulcaster's views about women's intellectual capacities were a commonplace and were repeated in, for example, Thomas Salter's *A mirror meet for all mothers, matrons and maidens* (1581), in which he urged that women should read edifying works, such as the lives of godly and virtous ladies taken from scripture or histories, but that a maid should be forbidden to read 'such books or ballads as may make her mind (being of itself very delicate) more feeble and effeminate'. By the last quarter of the sixteenth century books aimed specifically at a female readership were being printed in increasing numbers. This is indirect evidence that women's literacy rates were increasing and the implications of women's ownership of books is discussed later in this chapter.

Some of the books for women were deliberately simplified to cater for their presumed lack of scholarly learning. Thus Robert Cawdrey published a dictionary in 1604 for the use of 'Ladies and Gentlewomen, or any other unskillful persons' and authors deliberately wrote in English rather than Latin or Greek, assuming that women would not be able to read 'learned tongues'. Books for women included devotional works of religious guidance, prayers and meditations, practical books about cookery and needlework, herbals and medical works, guides to handwriting and model letter books, histories of women, conduct books and works on how to run households, such as Gervase Markham's *The English housewife* (1615), which was aimed at the woman who ran a family and 'hath her most general employments within the house'. Romances, fiction and other forms of literature were also aimed specifically at women, or were assumed to have a particular appeal to women (Hull 1982).

The closing of the convents at the Reformation had meant the loss of a number of centres where some young girls had received an education based on religion, morals, French and practical skills such as needlework. Convents made some provision for the training of novitiates, but they never took large numbers of other children as pupils and when they did so it was often an informal arrangement concerning one or two boys or girls. At the Reformation the largest number of girls being educated at any one convent was to be found at St Mary's Winchester, where in 1536 there were twenty six daughters of 'lords, knights and gentlemen'. Eileen Power described the establishment there as a 'fashionable seminary for young ladies'. She found no evidence, however, that nunneries ever functioned as day schools for poor local children and her conclusions on the educational influence of the nunneries were very pessimistic. Only a small proportion of the children of the upper classes were ever educated by nuns and the education that they received was very limited (Power 1922). There is scattered evidence that girls' boarding schools were being set up in the sixteenth century, perhaps to replace the educational provision of the convents. In the late sixteenth century, for example, there was a girls' school at Windsor run by a gentlewoman, but in general such establishments were scarce until the mid-seventeenth century (O'Day 1982).

Girls from wealthier families were more frequently taught either by tutors or governesses. Between 1547 and 1552 John Foxe the martyrologist was tutor to Lady Jane Howard and her sisters, and the daughters of Henry, Earl of Surrey. In the early seventeenth century

Lady Anne Clifford had the poet Samuel Daniel as one of her tutors, as well as a governess. It was also common for girls to be sent to other households to finish their education. In 1546 when she was nine, Lady Jane Grey joined the household of Queen Katherine Parr, and at the end of the sixteenth century the Countess of Huntingdon had a number of young women in her household, including Lady Margaret Hoby. Girls from aristocratic and gentry backgrounds would be taught skills relevant to their station in life while girls from poorer families were sent away from home as servants or apprenticed to learn either a trade or more commonly housewifery. The revision of the poor laws in Elizabeth's reign also provided for the apprenticeship of orphans and pauper children of both sexes with families in their parish (Gardiner 1929).

Evidence about the existence of schools specifically for girls in the period is scattered in a variety of sources. Women were occasionally presented to the Church courts for teaching without a licence, although whether they taught boys or girls is not often mentioned. From the early seventeenth century there is increasing evidence of the existence of girls' schools both in London and the provinces. There was Ladies Hall at Deptford, where the daughters of courtiers were educated and in 1617 they performed a masque for the queen, Anne of Denmark. In 1628 Mrs Freind was running a school at Stepney, where needlework, writing and music figured on the curriculum. Several schools were set up in Hackney by the 1630s and in his diary for May 1649 John Evelyn described travelling by barge to see the schools or colleges of young gentlewomen at Putney. There are sufficient references to similar schools in towns other than London for Rosemary O'Day to suggest that every town of any size had a girls' academy by the mid-seventeenth century (Gardiner 1929, O'Day 1982).

As Bathsua Makin's *Essay* of 1673 suggests, however, these schools did not teach the academic curriculum that was on offer in boys' grammar schools. In 1678 John Aubrey recorded that there were four or five boarding schools for girls in Oxford and he added condescendingly that 'the young ladies of London do learn as far as the rule of three and the rule of practice, and do find it to be a great use to them in buying of their silks, laces etc; but this belongs rather to a gynaceum' (Stephens 1972). After the Restoration more serious establishments were being set up by the Quakers and other dissenters and in 1686 the Bar Convent School was set up for Catholic girls in York. The Anglican Church was also active in setting up charity schools for orphans and poorer children to teach them basic literacy and practical skills such as sewing for the girls.

Yet, with so little systematic provision of education for girls, female literacy rates remained low throughout the early modern period. Cressy has argued that women were almost universally unable to sign their own names between 1500 and 1700. Using the ability to sign as an indicator of being able to both read and write, he has suggested that in 1500 only one per cent of women were fully literate as opposed to ten per cent of men. By 1640 the increase in ability to sign suggests that ten per cent of women and 30 per cent of men were literate. By 1720 the proportions had reached 25 for women and 45 for men. Only Londoners provided a dramatic exception to Cressy's pattern, and women in the capital may have reached rates of over 50 per cent literacy by the 1720s, partly because London possessed superior educational facilities for young women and partly because migration to London held attractions for women who were already well educated. Overall Cressy's figures support the argument that there was an increase in literacy in the period and that there was a faster growth in literacy amongst women than men (Cressy 1980).

The problems of using the evidence of signatures have been discussed in Chapter Three and Cressy's figures are most probably a considerable underestimate of the reading public at the time, because many individuals were taught to read but not to write (Spufford 1979). Evidence that a person can read is not so easy to detect as the ability to write, and therefore indirect measures of reading habits – such as book ownership or the increase in the circulation of printed books – must also be considered. Evidence taken from wills, inventories, letters and court cases shows that women from various social groups in the late fifteenth and early sixteenth centuries were acquiring books and set great store by them, both as items of social status and for their contents. Such evidence is not necessarily an indication that a book was read by an individual, but it is most unlikely that all such books remained unread by their female owners.

Peter Clark's study of probate inventories from Canterbury, Faversham and Maidstone shows that in the early seventeenth century 25 per cent of female testators and 40 per cent of male testators owned books. Religious works dominated the libraries examined by Clark, and the books owned by Alice Cornelius – a Canterbury widow who died in 1579 – might be taken as typical: a Bible, Erasmus's *Paraphrase*, a New Testament, a service book, and a volume of Augustine's

Meditations (Clark 1976). It is notable that Clark's figures are considerably higher than Cressy's percentages for literacy in the same period. This is because Clark's sample is limited to those wealthy enough to make wills, who were more likely to own books; and it may also reflect the higher literacy rates in towns.

Books that appear in inventories may not have been read by their owners at all – they may have been inherited or obtained as status symbols – but other types of evidence can help to indicate how women were using books in the period. Before the Reformation Lollard women are recorded as the owners of religious books and they were active in circulating them amongst the Lollard community. There is evidence that some of them memorized the ten commandments, the Lord's Prayer, *Ave Maria*, the Creed and the Epistles of St James and St Peter, which is a reminder that they were living in a predominantly oral society amd that it is possible to acquire and retain knowledge without the ability to either read or write (Cross 1978; McSheffrey 1995).

In the late fifteenth and early sixteenth centuries aristocratic women with court connections were the most common female owners of manuscripts and printed books, although the wives of London merchants are also recorded as book owners. Religious works were most popular amongst them, but there are also frequent references to romances and some histories. There is also evidence that books circulated amongst groups of women. When she died in 1495 Cicely Neville, Duchess of York, left a number of religious books as bequests to her granddaughters: Elizabeth of York, queen of Henry VII, received a psalter; Bridget, a Dominican nun, received copies of the *Golden legend*, the life of St Catherine and the visions of St Matilda; and Anne de la Pole, the prioress of the Bridgettine house of Syon, received a copy of St Bridget's *Revelations*. The Duchess also gave a breviary to Lady Margaret Beaufort, Henry VII's mother. Lady Margaret herself was a great patron of scholars and was described by her confessor John Fisher as 'right studious ... in books, which she had in great number both in English and in French', some of which she passed on to other female courtiers. She was also the translator of the fourth book of *The imitation of Christ* by Thomas à Kempis, which was printed in 1504 and was probably the first work to be published by a woman in England (Armstrong 1983; Mayor 1876; Jones & Underwood 1992; Meale 1993).

A generation or so later the learning of Henry VIII's queens,

41

Katherine of Aragon and Anne Boleyn, is well documented and it has been argued by Maria Dowling that the cultural links that they developed with scholars were of sufficient importance for them to rank as 'figures of European significance' in their patronage. Katherine was raised in the humanist tradition and pioneered women's education by commissioning the Spanish scholar, Juan Luis Vives, to devise an educational plan for her daughter Mary Tudor, which was published in 1524. Anne Boleyn's interests lay with the evangelical and Lutheran movements of the day, which later helped to contribute to her downfall. She kept a copy of Tyndale's 1534 New Testament open on a desk in her chamber so that the members of her household could read it and her chaplain, William Latymer, described her as 'very expert in the French tongue, exercising herself continually in reading the French Bible and other French books of like effect and conceived great pleasure of the same' (Dowling 1991).

The mastery of French, rather than Latin, would remain a neccesary accomplishment for women of high social status throughout the early modern period and in 1638 Lady Brilliana Harley wrote that she preferred to read 'anything in that tongue than in English'. Lady Harley's letters and commonplace books reveal that, in keeping with her puritan beliefs, she read mainly religious works including the *Bible*, Calvin's *Institutes*, and sermons and works of practical divinity by authors such as William Perkins. As the daughter of a courtier, she was also keenly interested in political news and received copies of speeches in Parliament and newsbooks from London whilst living in Herefordshire from the time of her marriage in 1623 to her death in 1643 (Lewis 1854; Eales 1990a).

Lady Harley not only acquired books of her own, but also had access to the extensive library owned by her husband. Other women more deliberately built up their own separate libraries. The books owned by Lady Ann Clifford were recorded in a particularly unusual way, as part of the background in the triptych portrait of her both as a young girl and in middle age. The painting, commissioned in 1646 and known as the 'Great Portrait' can still be seen on display in Appleby Castle and shows her surrounded by the works of Ovid, Boethius, Chaucer, Agrippa, Charron, Sidney, Spenser, Jonson and Donne amongst others. One of the largest libraries owned by a woman in the period was acquired by the Countess of Coventry, who listed hundreds of her books and plays in the early eighteenth century. By 1704 she owned works by Aphra Behn, Wycherley and Congreve, as well as poetry, sermons, history and political speeches and tracts (Perry 1986).

Another indicator of growing female literacy is the number of printed books written by women themselves. This was very restricted until the 1640s, but then started to increase with contributions from Lady Eleanor Davies, Margaret, Duchess of Newcastle, the Fifth Monarchist Anna Trapnel and the Quaker Margaret Fell amongst others. It was not, however, until the 1680s that the playwright Aphra Behn became the first Englishwoman who can be described as a professional author. Until the late 1560s most works by women were translations into English of religious works. In 1567 and 1573 Isabella Whitney, sister of the Cheshire-born lawyer Geoffrey Whitney, published two books of poetry and in 1578 Margaret Tyler published a translation of a Spanish romance. Aware of the warnings against women reading anything other than improving literature, Tyler wrote a vigorous defence of her subject matter. Men, she said, laid claim to being the sole possessors of knowledge, but if it was proper for men to write romances and dedicate them to women then it was fit for women to read them (Krontiris 1992; Ferguson 1985).

The novelty value of the female author was emphasized by Dorothy Leigh in her work of maternal advice, *The mother's blessing* of 1616, when she wrote that her work was something 'unusual among us'. The first four decades of the seventeenth century saw an increase in the number of original works by female authors. They were largely of a religious or literary nature and included domestic advice addressed to new mothers or to children. As Crawford has pointed out, religion and maternity were two areas where women could publish without upsetting conventional values (Crawford 1985).

In general early female authors mirrored the theories put forward by men, often lacing them with personal experiences that men did not have. In *The Countess of Lincoln's nursery* (1622) Elizabeth Clinton followed male authorities such as Vives, Sir Thomas Elyot and others in advising mothers to breastfeed their own children, rather than banish them to wet nurses. In her own case she was moved to write by conscience, because she had not always breastfed her own children. She advised women that 'we have followed Eve in transgression, let us follow her in obedience' by fulfilling the motherly duty of suckling children.

The posthumously published *The mother's legacy to her unborn child* (1624) written by Elizabeth Joceline shortly before her death in childbed is similarly traditionalist. Joceline had clearly assimilated the

43

precepts of the religious teaching she had received as a member of a clerical family. In the Approbation, or preface, of her book she was described as sparing in talking about her knowledge, 'possessing it, rather to hide, than to boast of'. In *The legacy* Joceline advised her husband that if their child was a girl then she should learn from the Bible 'as my sisters do' and 'housewifery, writing and good works: other learning a woman needs not', since often women ended up with more learning than wisdom. If her husband did want a learned daughter, then she prayed that God would give her 'a wise and religious heart, that she may use it to his glory, thy comfort and her own salvation'. *The legacy* was directed towards inculcating religious habits of prayer, meditation and sabbath observance in their child, who was warned against the sins of swearing, drunkenness, pride and malice. Joceline also emphasized the many snares set by the Devil to trap the unwary soul. Her book proved highly popular and went into seven impressions between 1624 and 1635.

Despite the increase in female authors in the seventeenth century, it was not until after the Restoration that women began to address the question of female education systematically in print. Bathsua Makin was the first Englishwoman to publish a sustained analysis of the benefits of improved education for women, along with a practical programme of schooling. She had acted as governess to Charles I's daughter Elizabeth in the 1640s and after the Restoration set up a school for girls outside London. She advertised the school in 1673 in her *Essay to revive the ancient education of gentlewomen,* which was dedicated to the future Queen Mary. Makin complained that 'the barbarous custom to breed Women low, is grown general amongst us' so that it was generally believed that women did not have the reason of men and were therefore unable to benefit from education. She called for a competent number of schools to be set up for girls and scorned those in existence, because for the most part they taught housewifery and little more. She cited examples of learned women from the Bible, classical history and recent times, noting that the Duchess of Newcastle 'by her own genius, rather than any timely instruction, over-tops many grave grown-men'.

Makin proposed that women should be taught 'Arts and Tongues', which would be of personal profit to them, but would also be advantageous to the nation by guarding against heresies and fallacies. Women's time would then be better employed than in dressing their hair and adorning their bodies whilst neglecting their souls. She argued that her scheme would allow women who worked as servants to choose better placements while married women would be of use to their husbands in their trades and better able to raise their children by good example. Widows would be able to understand and manage their own affairs. Makin emphasized that her intention was not to 'equalize women to men', for they were the weaker sex, although capable of 'impressions of great things'. The curriculum that she drew up for her school included dancing, music, singing, writing, keeping accounts, Latin, French, Hebrew and Greek, English grammar, astronomy, geography, arithmetic, history, experimental philosophy, natural history, painting, preserving, pastry-making and cookery.

Writing at the end of the century, Mary Astell agreed with Makin that it was tradition rather than nature that kept women in ignorance. In *A serious proposal to the ladies* (1694) she advanced her idea of a Protestant community or seminary for women where they could pursue a contemplative life and act charitably to others and thus stock the kingdom with 'pious and prudent' ladies. Religious books and philosophy, especially the French writers Descartes and Malebranche, would form their staple reading. Women, she argued, were as capable of learning as men, and she urged that women should be enabled to instruct their own sex at least. Her plans, she reassuringly wrote, did not extend to pretending that women should teach in Church or usurp authority, but only that women should be allowed to understand their own duties and not take them on trust from others.

Her suggestion had already been anticipated by a number of Restoration writers, including Clement Bardale, a schoolmaster, and the clergyman George Hickes, who asked his parishioners to give money to found colleges for women. The *Serious proposal* was well received amongst some of Astell's contemporaries, including John Evelyn who thought her writing to be 'sublime'. It also influenced a number of women such as Judith Drake, who wrote *An essay in defence of the female sex* (1696) and the poet Lady Mary Chudleigh, who acknowledged Astell as a source of inspiration. Although Mary Astell's seminary was never realized, she and some friends took the practical step of setting up a charity school for girls in Chelsea (Ferguson 1985; Perry 1986).

Even at the end of the seventeenth century there was clearly a perceived need for improved education for girls of all social classes. There had been a marked increase in the general level of literacy amongst women between 1500 and 1700, and in the formal educational provision available to girls of all classes. Starting from a lower base, the levels of female literacy increased at a faster rate than those of men, but nevertheless remained markedly lower. The increase in male literacy rates was a response to the growth in central and local government administration, the growing responsibilities placed on local magistrates by legislation in the period and the demand for better educated clergy and lawyers. The men of these classes wanted wives who were sufficiently educated to be suitable companions, and capable of looking after property and other concerns in their absence, but they saw no point in teaching their female relatives about the finer points of theology or the law.

The assumption that education for men and women had different aims and should be different in content remained largely unchanged throughout this period. In *Some thoughts concerning education* (1705) John Locke advised that 'the principal aim of my discourse is, how a young gentleman should be brought up from his infancy, which, in all things will not so perfectly suit the education of daughters; though where the difference of Sex requires different treatment, 'twill be no hard matter to distinguish' (Axtell 1968). In the main his contemporaries did not believe that the two sexes should receive similar education. The differences were to remain a matter of easy distinction to educationists until they were largely, but not entirely, removed by the later educational revolution of the mid-twentieth century.

CHAPTER SIX

Politics

The accessions of Mary Tudor, her sister Elizabeth and their cousin Mary Queen of Scots, raised questions in the mid-sixteenth century amongst contemporaries about the rights of women to inherit and exercise public office. This issue is of considerable interest to historians, but we should not overlook the fact that most of their opponents were concerned primarily with these queens' religious policies rather than their sex. The contention that as women they could not rule was ancillary to the wider political and confessional debate between Protestants and Catholics. Furthermore, these disputes should not eclipse the significance of more informal political networks in which women had always played a part. Barbara Harris has emphasized that political historians have traditionally concentrated on institutions which excluded women, such as the privy council, Parliament, the law courts and administrative bodies. They have thus created the impression that high politics were an exclusively male concern.

Harris has outlined the arenas in which elite women did participate actively in early Tudor politics. These include the household of the monarch and the court, as well as local patronage networks, which were often centred on the households of the aristocracy or local gentry (Harris 1990). The operation of national and local government was seen as part of the personal patronage of not only the monarchy but also powerful aristocratic and gentry families. This led to a considerable blurring of the boundaries between the public and private spheres and it was accepted that high ranking women could exert political or other influence on behalf of their husbands, sons or wider family and clientage networks. This was an important and well understood aspect of Tudor and Stuart administration and it extended to the attainment of offices, grants or favours from the monarch, and the exercise of influence over local officials.

The reigns of the Tudor and Stuart queens in England should thus properly be seen as an extension of the political activities of aristocratic and gentry women within their own family networks, in which blood ties and patronage links were all important to the exercise and accumulation of power. This point was acknowledged by Elizabeth's Secretary of State Sir Thomas Smith in his famous analysis of the English state, *De republica Anglorum*, written in the 1560s and first published in 1583, when he stated that:

> an absolute Queen, an absolute Duchess or Countess ... have that name, not by being married ... but by being the true, right and next successors in that dignity ... for the right and honour of the blood, and the quietness and suretie of the realm, is more to be considered than either the base age as yet impotent to rule, or the sex not accustomed (otherwise) to intermeddle with public affairs.

Fears that Mary Tudor's exercise of power might be suspect because of her sex were firmly addressed in 1554 when her position was clarified by a statute which stated that, although all previous statutes attributed royal authority to the king, the queen exercised it in 'as full, large and ample manner' as any of her predecessors (*SR* I Mary St. 3. c. 1. 2).

The publication at the end of her reign of John Knox's *The first blast of the trumpet against the monstrous regiment of women* (1558) constituted the fullest statement of the arguments against female rulers in the period. Knox was also concerned that the marriage of Mary Tudor to Philip of Spain, which had taken place in 1554, might mean that he would control the kingdom in order to aid Spanish interests. Susan Doran has shown that the question of marriage was also an important political concern in Elizabeth's reign when she continued serious marriage negotiations with foreign princes until she was in her late forties (Doran 1996).

Fears about these queens' marriages must be placed within the context of the religious conflict caused by the Reformation. The most vituperative denunciations of Mary Tudor came from Protestant exiles such as Knox, John Ponet and Christopher Goodman, agitating for her overthrow as a Catholic tyrant. Similarly the most virulent attacks on Elizabeth came from Catholic exiles such as William Allen, who hoped for a coalition between the papacy and the major European powers of Spain and France in order to replace her with a Catholic queen. The most hostile, and hence the most well known, attempt to discredit Mary Tudor because of her sex undoubtedly came from the pen of Knox. He held the extreme opinion that in comparison with men, women were not created in the image of God, and that women were not only subject to their husbands, they were subject to all men. This latter restriction was necessary because by their very nature women were 'weak, frail, impatient, feeble and foolish; and experience hath declared them to be inconstant, variable, cruel, and lacking the spirit of counsel and regiment'. For these reasons, argued Knox, women had been removed from authority in all ages and men who were influenced by their wives were thought to be unfit for public office. He agreed that women could inherit private possessions from their fathers, but not that they could inherit public offices (Shephard 1994).

Knox's work has been widely cited as evidence of the contemporary disapproval of female rulers, but *The first blast* was not simply an attack on women. It was one of a number of tracts written by Protestant exiles which associated Mary Tudor, as a Catholic, with the sin of idolatry. Knox followed earlier writers such as Ponet and Goodman in arguing that Mary should be overthrown because she was an idolatrous Catholic queen and their writings made a substantial contribution to the development of the political theory of resistance. Indeed Knox argued that a female ruler was herself an idol 'which hath the form and appearance but lacketh the virtue and strength which the name and proportion do resemble and promise'. Like other resistance theorists Knox drew a parallel between the rule of Mary Tudor and that of two idolatrous Old Testament queens, Athaliah and Jezebel, both of whom had to be slain before true religion could be restored to their kingdoms. Knox's tract was not therefore representative of universally held attitudes towards female rulers. This is illustrated by a number of authors who chose to rebut Knox's propositions.

The earliest reply to Knox came from another Protestant Marian exile, John Aylmer, entitled *An harborowe for faithfull and trewe subjects against the late blown blaste concerning the government of women* (1559), in which he defended Elizabeth's inheritance of the throne as God's will. Aylmer argued that the government of a woman was not unnatural and cited examples of earlier female rulers, but he was working within a traditional patriarchal framework and agreed that the rule of men was preferable to that of women. Richard Bertie, another Marian exile, wrote a manuscript at about the same time defending Elizabeth, and two Scottish Catholics, John Leslie and David Chambers, published defences of Mary Queen of Scots in 1569 and 1579 respectively. Leslie's work was specifically aimed at proving that Mary Stuart was rightful queen of England instead of Elizabeth, who was portrayed as illegitimate by her extreme Catholic opponents. As late as the early 1590s Lord Henry Howard, an English Catholic, wrote a manuscript in favour of Elizabeth and against Knox, in an attempt to rehabilitate himself at the English court after the execution of the Scottish queen in 1587. In her analysis of these five texts Amanda Shephard argues that Knox's opponents reached some radical conclusions about women including Lord Howard's argument that they could be educated for a public role (Shephard 1994).

Fears about women rulers need, therefore, to be balanced by the widely accepted contemporary arguments that all three queens had legitimate claims to the English monarchy. The statute of 1554 stressed that Mary Tudor was the undoubted 'heir and inheretrix' of the crown, thus by implication dismissing the rights of her main rival, Lady Jane Grey, who had recently been executed. This act did not say that any doubts about Mary had been raised because she was a woman, only that 'malicious and ignorant persons' might be persuaded into this 'error and folly' in the future. The principle of inheritance was all important to the landed classes who handed down power and wealth within their families from generation to generation, and any break in this principle would have had ramifications for the ruling elite as a whole. Mary had been treated as illegitimate by Henry VIII between 1533 and 1544, but at her accession in 1553 she found strong support from both the Catholic and Protestant aristocracy and gentry in England who wanted to see the principle of inheritance upheld. Elizabeth was similarly supported throughout her reign by both Catholic and Protestant nobles and gentry, despite her Protestant Settlement of the Church. Even if the establishment of the Tudor royal dynasty in 1485 had been accomplished by conquest, all of the Tudor monarchs relied on the argument of legitimate inheritance as the foundation of their claims to the throne.

The accessions of Mary Tudor and Elizabeth should not, therefore, be viewed as exceptional deviations from the political norm. They were instead an extension of both the principle of inheritance and of the acceptance that women could play a legitimate part in furthering the political interests of their families. Often the political participation of women took the form of involvement in marriage negotiations or of the exercise of patronage by a variety of means, but there are also some striking examples of the intervention of women at moments of political crisis in the century or so before Mary Tudor became queen. Aristocratic women were for example active in the defence of their family's political interests during the Wars of the Roses.

Margaret of Anjou played a prominent role in orchestrating the Lancastrian party after her husband, Henry VI, became increasingly incapacitated in the early 1450s, even to the extent of insisting that she should be treated as if she were the king in 1457 at Coventry. Cicely Neville, dowager Duchess of York, had what has been described by two modern historians as a 'commanding' influence within Yorkist circles, and her sons Edward IV and Richard, Duke of Gloucester, regularly consulted her on matters of state. From 1483 Lady Margaret Beaufort intrigued for the overthrow of Richard III and was ordered to be kept under house arrest by the king. Her personal connections with the Stanleys helped to sway the balance of forces at the battle of Bosworth in Henry Tudor's favour and she was subsequently the most prominent figure at court after her son, Henry VII. Beween 1499 and 1506 Lady Margaret's household at Collyweston acted as a regional royal council in the Midlands on his behalf. Here Margaret took an active role in sending orders to local officials, settling disputes and hearing judicial cases such as that concerning treasonable words against the king, which came before her in 1500 (Jones & Underwood 1992).

The active involvement of women in politics can also be seen during the reign of Henry VIII when his first wife, Katherine of Aragon, was appointed regent during his invasion of France in 1513 and the battle of Flodden was fought and won against the Scots under her aegis (*EBD*). Both Katherine and her successor, Anne Boleyn, were associated with political factions at court and a number of prominent women aligned themselves with one or other of these queens. Amongst those who opposed Henry VIII's divorce of Katherine were his own sister, Mary, Duchess of Suffolk, as well as Margaret Pole, Countess of Salisbury (whose sons had a claim to the throne), and Elizabeth, Duchess of Norfolk, who was banned from the court for speaking too freely about the divorce.

A number of women openly opposed the Henrician Reformation and Lady Margaret Bulmer suffered the penalty of burning for her support for the Pilgrimage of Grace, the major armed revolt which took place in 1536, while Margaret Pole was executed for treason in 1541. Katherine, dowager Duchess of Suffolk, was a prominent supporter of the Protestant cause and in 1547, two years after her husband's death, was described as ruling all Lincolnshire. Not only was she a member of Henry VIII's inner circle in the final months of his life, but she also successfully cultivated links with the Lord Protector, Edward, Duke of Somerset, and his duchess, Anne, during the reign of Edward VI. During Mary's reign the duchess fled into exile with her second husband Richard Bertie. On her return at the start of Elizabeth's reign she continued to use her influence on behalf of Protestant reform (Harris 1990).

Such high-profile activity was complemented in the late middle ages and the early modern period by the integration of elite women into more routine aspects of politics. Tudor and Stuart politics were primarily conducted through the exercise of patron–client relationships, which often originated in – or were cemented by – marriage alliances. In this respect women had a very important role as mediators between different kinship networks. The marriage in 1545 between William Cecil, later Lord Burghley, and Mildred, daughter of Sir Anthony Cooke, helped to forge a formidable family network of Elizabethan courtiers and local administrators. Mildred's sister Ann married Sir Nathaniel Bacon and was mother to Sir Francis Bacon. Their youngest sister, Elizabeth, married first Sir Thomas Hoby and secondly John, Lord Russell. Lady Russell made frequent use of her connections with the Cecils and her demands reflect the function of personal and family advancement as an integral part of the political process at the time. In 1596, Lady Russell wrote to her nephew Sir Robert Cecil, then secretary of state, recommending the Earl of Kent as Lord President of the Council in the North. A little later she asked Sir Robert to make one of her clients, Mr Dale, Master of Requests and in 1597 she approached Sir Robert to further her plans to marry her daughter Ann to Lord Herbert, son of the Earl of Worcester. Lady Russell proposed to settle £2,000 on her daughter over a ten-year period and observed shrewdly that it would 'be a sufficient portion for an Earl of so small revenue and so many children'. Sir Robert Cecil's father, Lord Burghley had earlier been instrumental in the negotiations which led to the marriage between Lady Russell's son Thomas Posthumous Hoby and the heiress Margaret Dakins in 1595 (Meads 1930).

In 1613 Frances Howard's divorce from her first husband, the Earl of Essex, was vigorously supported by her influential Howard relatives, including her father, the Earl of Suffolk, and her great-uncle, the Earl of Northampton, because it would enable her to marry her lover and royal favourite, Robert Carr, to the furtherance of the Howard connection. In 1623 Sir Robert Harley was prepared to accept a relatively low dowry of £1,600 on marrying the daughter of the secretary of state, Sir Edward Conway, in part because of the political advantages of the match (Lindley 1993; Eales 1990a).

Elite women were also actively involved in dispensing patronage to artists, writers and clergymen, whose artistic and literary creations served to magnify the wealth and position of their patrons and their families. After the death of her brother Sir Philip Sidney in 1586, Mary, Countess of Pembroke, continued to support members of his literary circle, including Samuel Daniel the poet, who was employed at her residence at Wilton as tutor to her elder son in the 1590s. The countess's patronage and her own writing, including the completion of a metrical translation of the psalms originally started by Sidney, linked her to the promotion of the Calvinist cause in England. Her interests extended to chemical and scientific enquiry and she supported the work of a number of male practioners including Adrian Gilbert. Lady Mary Vere, whose husband commanded the English volunteer force in the Palatinate in the early 1620s, was also strongly associated with the Calvinist wing of the English Church through her support for a number of puritan clergy (Beilin 1987; Hannay 1997; Eales 1990a).

During the reigns of both Mary and Elizabeth the influence of female courtiers was greatly increased when women from favoured aristocratic and gentry families replaced male officials as the monarch's personal attendants in the royal household. At the same time there was a new separation between membership of the household and the great offices of state, which remained a male preserve. In Elizabeth's reign the ladies of the Privy Chamber were drawn mainly from families who had blood relationships with the Tudors, including the Howards, Careys, Radcliffes and Knollys. It was reported at the beginning of Elizabeth's reign that in order to keep political factions at arm's length, she would not discuss business with the ladies of her household. Elizabeth certainly punished independent initiative by these women if she disapproved of it and in 1562 she placed two long-serving members of her household, Catherine Asteley and Dorothy Bradbelte, under house arrest for writing to the King of Sweden about her marriage plans.

Elizabeth did, however, make use of her ladies-in-waiting for political purposes. In 1559 Mary Sidney, the sister of Lord Robert Dudley, was used by Elizabeth as a go-between in her marriage negotiations with Archduke Charles of Austria. Elizabeth also allowed the Ladies of the Privy Chamber to press the suits of male relatives and confidants. Robert Dudley, Earl of Leicester was thus able to make use of his sister and other female associates in the Privy Chamber, including Blanche Parry and Dorothy Bradbelte, as a route of access to the queen. Leicester also cultivated contacts with Dorothy, Lady Stafford, who wrote to the sheriff of Norfolk in 1576 asking him to appoint one of the earl's men as under-sheriff in the county and assuring him that she would return the favour. In the aftermath of the execution of Mary Queen of Scots in 1587, Lord Burghley was able to use Frances, Lady Cobham as a direct channel of information about Leicester's efforts to avoid blame. In the second part of Elizabeth's reign Mary, Lady Scudamore acted as a point of contact in Elizabeth's household for the Sidneys, and for the earls of Shrewsbury and Rutland (Murphy 1987; Doran 1996; Wright 1987).

Following Elizabeth's death such close lines of communication between female courtiers and the monarch were closed off and separate royal households were set up for the queens of James I and Charles I, Anne of Denmark and Henrietta Maria, both of whom attracted ladies-in-waiting who were nevertheless politically ambitious. Amongst Queen Anne's ladies the most influential was Lucy, Countess of Bedford, who has been described by Barbara Lewalski as 'a power to be reckoned with in the disposition of offices, the arrangement of marriages and the shaping of Jacobean cultural life'. Her residence at Twickenham was a resort for the writers and artists whom she patronized including John Donne, Ben Jonson, George Chapman, Samuel Daniel and John Dowland. She also influenced the development of court masques through her own participation in them and her patronage of Jonson and other masque writers. In 1618 John Pory advised Sir Dudley Carleton to make his request for court office through 'mylady of Bedford (who is above measure powerful with both the Marquesses and mylord Chamberlain)' (Lewalski 1987).

The traditional pattern of politics was disturbed in the mid-seventeenth century by the outbreak of the civil wars and the brief establishment of a republic in England. The years from 1640 to 1660 were a period when many women took an overtly active role in political affairs. Henrietta Maria was rumoured to be in danger of attainder by

Parliament early in January 1642 and this may have triggered Charles I's attempt to arrest the five leading members of the House of Commons in order to thwart their plans against his wife. The Queen's parliamentarian opponents erroneously believed she was responsible for a Catholic plot to subvert the Protestant religion and destroy the English constitution. In response to the growing political crisis Henrietta Maria fled abroad to raise money and troops for the royalist cause from France and Holland. She received little aid and returned to England to give moral support to the king's war effort. The exiled royal court was a centre of political intrigue in which women participated as channels of covert information. Lady Ann Fanshawe recorded that in 1644 when she was at the royalist headquarters in Oxford a number of women, including Lady Rivers, Lady Isabella Thynne and Lady d'Aubigny were involved in passing on intelligence (Loftis 1979). Lady d'Aubigny was particularly celebrated in court circles because she had recently escaped being court-martialled by Parliament for her role in Waller's plot.

Another noted intelligence gatherer was Lucy Hay, Countess of Carlisle, who used her position at the court of Charles I to feed information to Parliament in the critical period at the end of 1641 and early 1642. She has been portrayed as a treacherous turncoat, but Ann Hughes has pointed out that there was a coherent political policy behind her actions. The countess was closely associated with the anti-Spanish group at court headed by her brother and brother-in-law, the earls of Northumberland and Leicester. Immediately before the outbreak of the Civil Wars her sympathies lay with the establishment of a strongly Protestant monarchy with powers curtailed by the aristocracy (EBD).

The Civil Wars also affected people at every level of society and provoked the largest mass demonstrations by women in the period. The first was on 31 January 1642 when a company of women delivered a petition to the House of Lords complaining of the decay of trade and demanding an end to religious disputes and the relief of Protestants in Ireland after the recent insurrections. Hostile observers at the time certainly tried to discredit the petitions by alleging they were written by men and that the petitioners were women of low character. In August 1643, when groups of two to three thousand women converged on Parliament to petition for peace, the supporters of the war branded the women as the 'inferior sort', 'whores', 'the scum of the suburbs' and an 'abundance of Irish women'. In 1649 when women petitioned for the release of four Leveller leaders, the Speaker of the House of Commons sent them a message that 'the matter you petition about is of an higher concernment than you understand' (Higgins 1973).

These petitions were satirized in ribald pamphlets that purported to come from women, with such titles as *The parliament of women* (1646) or the *Virgins complaint* (1646). The republican Henry Neville wrote three such squibs, *The ladies parliament* and *The ladies, a second time, assembled* in 1647 and *The commonwealth of ladies* in 1650. In the last of these Neville caricatured the prominent ladies of the royalist court, including Lady Isabella Thynne, Lady Montague and Lady Craven, who had assembled to discuss 'the common enemy' – their husbands (Fraser 1984). Despite the propaganda treatment of the women's petitions, they should not be interpreted as objects of universal derision and they did draw sympathetic support from some quarters. The royalist Earl of Clarendon later described the peace protesters of 1643 as the wives of substantial citizens, who had more courage than their menfolk (Higgins 1973).

The actions of the demonstrators should be considered within the context of women's widespread involvement in earlier religious or economic demonstrations throughout the period. Women were actively involved in pulling down enclosures in the sixteenth and seventeenth centuries and it has been suggested that women were present in almost every food riot of the period aimed at overpricing or shortages, in which matters women were perceived to have a special interest and knowledge (Walter 1980; Houlbrooke 1986). Ann Hughes has demonstrated that the petitions from Leveller women similarly emphasized that they had a right to be heard in defence of their homes and families. There is no conclusive evidence that women wrote all or any of the petitions they presented. They have been analyzed in detail by Patricia Higgins, who has pointed out that the petitions all used the language of submission. Thus the petitioners were described as the 'weaker sex', who were following the example of men, but they also developed a series of justifications for the rights of women to petition and to demonstrate. In July 1653 when twelve female petitioners led by the sectary Katherine Chidley were told that that 'they being women, and many of them wives, so the law took no notice of them', they replied that some of them were not wives and pressed for their petition to be received by Parliament.

Many of the women's petitions justified the right to address Parliament by reference to Biblical or historical heroines and even to the fate of the female Marian martyrs at Smithfield. The Leveller petitions also transferred claims of equality from the religious arena to the secular sphere: thus a petition of April 1649 argued that women had 'an equal share and interest with men in the commonwealth' and in May 1649 another petition justified the rights of women by asserting that women were created in the image of God and had an 'interest in Christ equal unto men' while also referring to their political and legal rights enshrined in the Petition of Right of 1628 and 'other good laws of the land' (Hughes 1995; Higgins 1973).

There is also scattered evidence of women taking part in local parliamentary elections. During the 1550s, while her son was a minor, the widowed Dame Elizabeth Copley nominated the two members of Parliament for the rotten borough of Gatton where the Copleys owned the lordship. The right of her daughter-in-law, Catherine, to the nomination was a legal part of her widow's jointure and it was only overturned by the privy council in 1586 when it became clear that she was a Catholic. Dame Dorothy Packington exercised a similar right for the borough of Aylesbury in 1572 and as Sir John Neale observed 'it was not the sex, but the lordship of the borough that mattered' (Neale 1949). During the Long Parliament elections of 1640 Lady Unton Dering helped to organize the campaign of her husband, Sir Edward Dering, to be elected as one of the knights of the shire for Kent. In her letters to her husband she reported who had declared suppport for him, including the Dean of Canterbury Cathedral, Isaac Bargrave, and warned him of the double dealing of Sir Edward Boys, who 'professes to be for you, yet he works earnestly for some other underhand whom he will not name publicly' (Cresswell 1994).

Similarly Lady Brilliana Harley co-ordinated her son's campaign in the Hereford by-election in the summer of 1642. Her letters reveal how she drew on her local contacts: thus she recorded that she had written to 'my cousin Elton, for his daughter has married Mr Weaver's son and young Weaver has power over many voices. Doctor Wright persuaded me to write to my cousin Vaughan, who has interest in some of [the] aldermen'. Lady Harley gracefully halted her efforts on hearing of a rival candidate, Viscount Scudamore's son, who had better connections with the city of Hereford and whose election was secure. Lady Harley's energetic channeling of information about the political and religious divisions in Herefordshire to her husband at Westminster and her determined defence of her home against royalist siege in

1643 should not, therefore, be seen as an extraordinary response by a woman to the growing crisis of civil war. Rather these activities should be interpreted as the logical extension of her concern to maintain Harley family influence in the county in time of war as well as in peace (Eales 1990a).

After the Restoration the traditional pattern of court and local politics was re-established, providing areas in which elite women such as Lady Rachel Russell and Sarah Churchill continued to influence the political process to the advantage of their personal and family affairs. One crucial difference after the Civil Wars was the gradual development of political groupings in the forms of the Whig and Tory parties, which also attracted political demonstrations from women lower down the social scale. The most well documented attempts by a female courtier to influence high politics in the early modern period were made in the reign of Queen Anne by Sarah Churchill, Duchess of Marlborough, who was appointed groom of the stole, mistress of the robes and keeper of the privy purse on the accession of Anne in 1702. Sarah started her court career in 1673 in the household of James II's queen, Mary of Modena, when she was an attendant on the then Princess Anne. Sarah's influence over Anne was considerable and in 1689 extended to persuading the princess to recognize the coup against her father and to accept the joint accession of William III and Mary II. The reigns of Mary and later of her sister Anne did not provoke the criticism of female rule that had been levelled earlier by John Knox at Mary Tudor. This was partly because Elizabeth I's reign was still seen as a golden age and also because the political opponents of the two queens preferred to attack them as usurpers of the power of their father, James II (Schwoerer 1988, Claydon 1996).

Sarah Churchill gradually lost favour during Anne's reign, largely through her support for Whig politicians in defiance of the queen's Tory leanings; and in 1711 both Sarah and her husband resigned their court offices. This did not prevent Sarah from continuing to take an active role in local politics where she campaigned vigorously in parliamentary elections through the use of agents and letter writing. Her initial involvement in local elections had started when her husband was absent on military campaigns between 1702 and 1711, but his stroke in 1716 and death in 1722 gave her greater freedom to wield influence. The barriers that Sarah encountered to her own ambitions were expressed in the comment she made in 1714 that 'I am confident I should have been the greatest hero that ever was known in the Parliament House, if I had been so happy to have been a man' (Harris 1983, 1991).

Sarah Churchill's ambitions were unusually clearly stated and well documented, but in keeping with the activities of women throughout the period they were an accepted extension of the political interests of a male relative. All too often, however, women's political activities have been trivialized as 'petticoat politics', or openly derided as ineffective or as evidence of feminine manipulation. In fact women's political activities differed very little from those of men. On both sides powerful individuals were concerned to secure the success of their own family or patronage networks and this is an area in which the participation of women still awaits further serious detailed and systematic research.

CHAPTER SEVEN

The family

Early modern theorists believed that women's proper sphere was the family where they could fulfil their roles as dutiful daughters, wives and widows. The advice in conduct books and the educational theories about women were largely based on the assumption that they would marry and raise a family of their own. These beliefs were reinforced by medical thinking about the biological nature of women, who were thought to be at risk of severe physical and mental illness if they did not engage in regular sexual relations (Eccles 1982). This dovetailed with the popular belief that women were sexually voracious, which surfaced in ribald ballads and the more misogynistic literature of the day. Moralists and medical writers argued that women's sexuality should be satisfied within the bounds of marriage and in *The woman's doctor* (1652) Nicholas Fontanus argued that 'wives are more healthful than widows or virgins, because they are refreshed with the man's seed and ejaculate their own, which being excluded, the cause of the evil is taken away'.

Despite these assumptions, marriage patterns were governed by economic conditions and a large proportion of the population never married, in part because of the expense of setting up a new household. Women's experience of family life varied considerably according to their social class, which affected their age at first marriage, the frequency of their pregnancies, their chances of remarriage as widows and the size of their households. At all social levels, however, women were active participants in the process of family formation and in the rituals which marked important life-cycle events such as marriage, birth and death (Cressy 1997; Hallam 1996).

Statistics about marriage formation and sexual behaviour in this period can never be absolutely accurate, because of the absence of complete data. It has been estimated, however, that in the late sixteenth and seventeenth centuries the percentage of the population which remained unmarried varied from between four and five per cent to perhaps as much as 25 per cent, with the highest levels coinciding with a period when real wages fell sharply in the first half of the seventeenth century (Wrigley & Schofield 1989). Not surprisingly, illegitimacy rates also peaked at about the same time and at their highest, around 1600, represented at least 4.5 per cent of all births. Overall illegitimacy accounted for between 1.5 per cent and 2 per cent of births in the years 1500-1700 and it was regarded by contemporaries as a problem affecting the poorer ranks in society.

Adair's research, based on baptismal records, has revealed considerable regional variations in the incidence of illegitimacy throughout the period, with the highest levels in the north-west and the lowest in the east and south-east of England. Although these may have been caused by economic considerations, Adair suggests that different patterns of courtship played a part, with greater acceptance of trial marriage or lengthy courtship in the highland regions than in the lowlands. Attempts to detect and punish bastardy and other illicit sexual behaviour became more energetic in the late sixteenth and early seventeenth centuries, although this too was subject to regional variations. The crackdown on extra-marital sex and other disorders has been associated with the spread of puritanism, but those areas most affected by economic pressures often proved more active in prosecuting offenders in order to prevent the poor from having children they could not support (Laslett 1977; Adair 1996; Quaife 1979; Ingram 1987).

Single women did not necessarily have more freedom than wives since most unmarried girls, below the wealthiest classes, were sent as servants or apprentices to other houses where they were part of the household of their masters. The diarist Samuel Pepys, for example, took in his unmarried sister Paulina on the basis that she came 'not as a sister in any respect but as a servant' and was not to eat with him and his wife. This was unusual treatment of a sibling, although the presence of more distant blood relatives as servants in the home was a common practice. Pepys' worries about Paulina's future as an unmarried woman were, however, common enough and eventually she found a husband (Eales 1992).

In the period 1550–1700 the median age at first marriage for women varied between 26.0 and 26.8. In the same period men's median age at first marriage fell from 29.3 to 27.9. This relatively late marriage pattern reflected the economic constraints that were caused by both population growth and the inflation of the period. The wealthier members of society were not so directly affected by these considerations and could afford to create separate households at an earlier age. Amongst the landed elite marriage was a transaction which could bring with it political connections and social status and the earlier a match was concluded the sooner such advantages could be realized. Stone has estimated that for women of the upper landed classes the average age at first marriage was 20 in the late sixteenth century, rising to 22 by the late seventeenth century; and for eldest sons the respective figures were 22 and 24 (Wrigley & Schofield 1989; Stone 1977).

The fact that aristocrats and gentlewomen tended to marry earlier than other women meant they were also likely to have more pregnancies, although the Countess of Lincoln, who contracted her marriage at the age of ten and bore eighteen children, was an extreme example. It was also more probable that wealthy women would remarry if they were widowed. The three marriages of Lady Margaret Hoby, who first married when she was 15, and the four marriages of Elizabeth Talbot, Countess of Shrewsbury, who first married when she was 14, were thus unusual, but not remarkable (*EBD*). Richer women also presided over larger domestic establishments consisting of servants, some of whom might have been kin, and relatives such as elderly parents, unmarried siblings and children, including step-children, nephews, nieces or wards. Most historians would agree that these extended groupings were generally to be found amongst the elite and that the most common household form in England amongst the rest of society was the nuclear family of parents and children (Macfarlane 1978; Laslett 1983; Houlbrooke 1984).

Lawrence Stone's research on the family has been particularly controversial, since he has argued that affection within families was lacking in the early modern period. He linked the growth of loving relationships to the emergence of the nuclear family, which he placed later than most historians, from the mid-seventeenth century onwards. Stone's study was confined largely to aristocratic and gentry families, for which he set out three separate stages of development. The first phase was the 'open lineage family', in evidence between 1450 and 1630, in which extended kinship networks were important, and emotional ties between husbands and wives and their children were weak. A transition ocurred between 1550 and 1700 when the nuclear family became more resistant to the influence of the extended family and there was greater evidence of private family affection. Finally the years 1640-1800 witnessed the emergence of what Stone termed the 'closed, domesticated nuclear family', in which there was warmth and emotional commitment while the role of extended kinship was considerably reduced (Stone 1977).

Stone has been criticized for adopting a 'masculine and elitist' perspective, which treats women of all social classes in a perfunctory manner, and for concentrating only on the upper ranks of society. His methodology has also been questioned, because the sources he used, such as private letters, diaries and autobiographies, became steadily more abundant in this period. This alone may account for the apparent increase in expressions of fondness within families at the time (Schwoerer 1984). In contrast, historians working on the history of the family below gentry level are faced with a dearth of such intimate material and have had to reconstruct family units using less personal sources such as parish registers, census lists and tax records. Because of gaps in these documents it is not always easy to reach general conclusions. Only 15 per cent of parishes, for example, have records of baptisms, marriages and burials dating back to 1538, the first date of registration, and even then the information they contain is not always complete. There are considerable gaps during the 1640s and 1650s as a result of the Civil Wars and the introduction of civil registration.

Nevertheless, the pattern which emerges from such documents shows that during the sixteenth and seventeenth centuries the majority of households below gentry level were headed by an individual or by a couple and that households containing two or more couples were unusual. One major drawback of such evidence is that it rarely gives any insight into the influence of the wider kinship group upon the nuclear family. Indeed it cannot be relied upon even to identify the extent of kinship networks in the way that documentation for elite families, such as heralds' visitations or wills, can be used to uncover complex webs of cousinage. A second problem is that it does not illustrate the nature of personal relationships within the nuclear family. These defects have been partially addressed by historians using evidence from court cases of marital disputes and litigation over wills in order to assess contemporary expectations of family life (Houlbrooke 1979; Ingram 1987; O'Hara 1991; Gowing 1996).

The formation of a new family unit through marriage was an event that concerned not only the couple themselves, but also their immediate families and the wider community. Amongst the aristocracy and greater gentry the arrangement of a marriage was primarily seen as a legal and economic undertaking, in which the two family groups and their advisers negotiated a series of financial settlements before the match took place. These would include the size of the dowry to be paid by the bride's family, as well as arrangements for the groom's family to provide a jointure, usually consisting of an income from land, and accomodation for the wife if she were widowed. Marriages were arranged with an eye to the financial advantages of the dowry and the social benefits of an alliance with a prominent family. At this social level parents expected to play a major role in the choice of a partner for their children and often took the initiative in suggesting a match directly to other parents, even before the prospective bride and groom had met each other (Houlbrooke 1984). Under these conditions it was not uncommon for negotiations to break down, either because one side felt slighted by the other's financial offerings or because one of the couple refused the match.

It was widely held by the early seventeenth century that children should not be forced into an unwanted partnership. The story of Elizabeth Paston, who for the space of three months was beaten 'once in the week or twice, sometimes twice in one day, and her head broken in two or three places' for refusing an arranged marriage in the mid-fifteenth century is an extreme case (Bennett 1968). The sentiments of Katherine, dowager Duchess of Suffolk, who wrote in 1550 to William Cecil about her son's marriage were more common. Although the duchess wished the daughter of the Duke of Somerset to marry her son, she confessed that 'I am not ... desirous that she should be constrained by her friends to have him' and hoped that the couple would 'begin their loves of themselves, without our forcing'. In the mid-1630s Lucy Hutchinson was able to refuse 'many offers', which her mother and friends thought advantageous and to marry the man of her choice. Lucy described herself as 'obedient, loath to displease them, but more herself, in marrying such as she could find no inclination to' (Wood 1846; Sutherland 1973).

Women often took a prominent role in initial marriage negotiations, especially if they were widows such as the Duchess of Suffolk or Lucy Hutchinson's mother and were acting on behalf of their children. Other female relatives also played an active part. In 1623 Sir Edward Conway recorded that his sister-in-law, Lady Vere, had first suggested the possibility of a match between his daughter, Brilliana, and the Herefordshire gentleman, Sir Robert Harley. Lady Vere analyzed the advantages of the marriage in terms both of personal affection and wealth, and acquainted Conway with Harley's affection for Brilliana and 'laid before me his parentage, the abilities of his mind, his ripe discretion, his well grounded religion', not forgetting to add the value of the Harley estates (BL Add. MSS 61989/81). Lady Vere's efforts were successful and the couple married later that year after Conway had made a thorough investigation into the Harley family's financial standing (Eales 1990a).

Lower down the social scale, family and friends also felt that they should be consulted in order to ensure the social and economic suitability of a match. Disputes in the Church courts about the contracting of marriage usually involved the middling ranks of society and they reveal that at this social level marriages were entered into for love as well as monetary considerations, and that clandestine marriages took place without the sanction of parents. Ingram cites a Wiltshire case of 1588 in which a couple admitted 'they did well fancy one the other' and a case in 1615 when Abigail Smith was described as 'sicklow . . . for love' of William Head. Where objections from family and friends were encountered they often centred on social differences between the couple. Relatives could use monetary threats, including disinheritance, in order to prevent what they saw as an uneven match.

The Church court records also show that as long as a relationship ended in marriage within a reasonable space of time, a good deal of latitude was given to courting couples, which was not the case at the higher social levels. Accordingly, as many as 25 per cent of brides were pregnant at the time of marriage in the later sixteenth century. This figure dropped to 16.2 per cent in the second half of the seventeenth century, perhaps as a result of an increase in prosecutions, although Ingram argues that there was little disgrace attached to the condition as long as the parents were intending to marry. The high incidence of pre-nuptial pregnancy also reflects the popular belief that an undertaking to marry made before witnesses was legally binding (Outhwaite 1995; Ingram 1987; Hair 1966–7, 1970; Wrigley & Schofield 1989).

The choice of a marriage partner was clearly one which balanced the affections and desires of the couple with the social and economic expectations of their relatives and friends. The remarriage of a widow or widower was an occasion when they could make a freer choice. In 1535 the widowed Mary Boleyn secretly married William Carey and justified her actions to her sister Anne and Henry VIII by arguing that 'love overcame reason; and for my part I saw so much honesty in him, that I loved him as well as he did me' (Wood 1846). Despite Stone's arguments to the contrary, the existence of such emotional ties both before and within marriage is well documented. Jennifer Ward found that, for the late middle ages, the letters of the Paston family in Norfolk and of the Stonor family in Oxfordshire show that affection existed between married couples and argues that such love was probably widespread, even if it was also based on economic considerations. The letters of Honor, Lady Lisle written to her husband in 1538 and 1539 also convey an impression of intimacy between the couple (Ward 1992; St Clare Byrne 1981).

The letters of Lady Brilliana Harley to her husband Sir Robert, which span a twenty-year period from their marriage in 1623 to her death in 1643, are similarly revealing of an enduring relationship based on affection as well as on financial, social and political expediencies. There is also evidence of the dynamics involved in maintaining a deferential relationship while being expected to act on behalf of a husband in his absence. Lady Harley followed the advice of the conduct books in always addressing her husband, who was nearly twenty years her senior, respectfully as 'Sir' or 'Dear Sir', but her letters also reveal a loving and humorous relationship. In 1626, when Sir Robert was in London attending Parliament, she wrote: 'I am so much pleased with this silent discoursing with you, that as I spent part of the morning in this kind of being with you, so now I begin the night with it and in these lines receive the remembrance of my love, of which you have not a part but all' (BL Add. MSS 70110). In 1641, after eighteen years of marriage, she described Sir Robert as 'the comfort of my life'.

During Harley's absences Lady Brilliana had considerable freedom in ordering her household, arranging the education of her sons, despatching her daughter to Lady Vere's home and overseeing the running of the estates. Between 1640 and 1643 as civil war broke out, she also kept him fully and perceptively informed about political and religious developments in their county. Nevertheless, she appeared deferential in asking for his opinions before she took any major decisions. When Sir Robert counselled her not to leave their house when the war broke out in 1642, she remained in Herefordshire despite her fears and her correct prognosis that their home would be besieged by royalist forces. After the siege had been lifted in the autumn of 1643 Harley finally agreed that his wife and children should come to London, but having successfully organized a six week defence against the enemy, Lady Harley politely refused his advice on the grounds that her presence was necessary to preserve the influence of the Harley family in the region (Eales 1990a).

Lady Harley's decision raises questions about how far women acknowledged the precepts of the conduct books and accepted their husbands' authority within the home. In 1617, after some fifty years of marriage, Lady Grace Mildmay wrote a remarkable meditation on the corpse of her husband, Sir Anthony, before his burial in which she reflected that 'I carried always that reverent respect towards him, in regard of my good conceit which I ever had of the good parts which I knew to be in him, that I could not find in my heart to challenge him for the worst word or deed which ever he offered me in all his life: as to say why spake you this, or why did you that, but in silence passed over all such matters betwixt us. So that we are parted in all love and christian charity, until our happy meeting in heaven'. Lady Mildmay also copied out exhortations to wives derived from St Paul in her private papers and she clearly believed, in evaluating her married life at its end, that she had obeyed them (Pollock 1993).

In contrast, Alison Wall has detected a tendency to subvert the rhetoric of female submissiveness in the letters of Joan and Maria Thynne to their husbands, John and Thomas. Whereas Joan agreed in 1575 at the age of 16 to marry her husband without having met him, Maria contracted a clandestine marriage with her husband in 1594, which the Thynne family tried to have annulled. As their marriages progressed both women took on increasing responsibilities on behalf of their husbands in running the Longleat estates and, like Lady Harley, both women proved to be capable managers. Wall concludes that the Thynne women were assertive and independent, that they were neither submissive nor shrews and that they 'shared responsibility in amicable partnerships' with their husbands (Wall 1990).

One of the most detailed and frank descriptions of an early modern marriage was written by the dissenting minister Richard Baxter, whose wife Margaret came from a gentry rather than a clerical family. It is clear from his account that Margaret's social background made her highly assertive in her dealings with her husband as well as with outsiders, although she was careful to use religious scruple as her justification. Baxter was painfully honest about the ways in which she openly criticized him for writing too much and not spending enough time with her and their household in religious observances. She also chided him for conforming to the established Church in reading the

Lord's Prayer. The social mismatch of their backgrounds was apparent in their attitudes towards their servants. Margaret set them to washing the stairs and the rooms, while her husband 'thought that . . . so much ado about cleanliness and trifles was a sinful curiosity'. Baxter's conclusion about marriage was most unusual for a Protestant cleric for he decided after his wife's death in 1681 that ministers should not marry at all (Eales 1990b).

However mismatched the Baxters may have been, there was no possibility that they could divorce. It was possible to have a marriage annulled by the Church courts on the gounds of non-consummation, prior contract to another party or consanguinity (a blood relationship between the couple). Beyond that a spouse could sue in the Church courts for a formal separation from bed and board on the grounds of ill-treatment, but even if the suit was successful it would not allow either party to remarry. An informal system of separation also existed when a husband or wife simply left the marital home and one or both parties then remarried illegally. A sample of such cases from the Canterbury diocesan courts from the years 1559–65 illustrates the penalties meted out by the Church for such moral offences. Joan Ramesdale of Canterbury admitted that she had remarried while her first husband was still alive and was ordered to perform penance. Katherine Moswell was prosecuted for not living with her husband and was excommunicated after she did not appear in court. Walter Colton was accused of having two wives, but admitted in court to having no less than four, although two were very probably dead; he was warned not to keep company with his fourth wife and was sentenced to perform penance (Willis 1975).

Stone calculated that, between 1570 and 1659, ten per cent of the marriages of the peerage ended in annulment, separation or estrangement. Ingram has found that the poor were also vulnerable to broken marriages, citing a survey of the poor in Norwich of about 1570 which showed that eight per cent of the married women had allegedly been deserted by their husbands. For the middling sort, concerns of property were clearly powerful incentives in keeping marriages stable, although the number of unhappy marriages which did not surface in the courts or in other documents can only be a matter of conjecture (Stone 1977; Ingram 1987). Another factor to be considered was the mortality rate, as some marriages did not last long enough for the partners to fall out and seek solace elsewhere.

Pregnancy in particular carried with it a one per cent risk of maternal death and since women on average could expect to have six or seven live children during their childbearing years they were particularly sensitive to the fears of death that pregnancy provoked (Pollock 1990). Elizabeth Jocelin's foreboding of death before the birth of her only child was accompanied by the secret purchase of her own winding sheet. She died in 1622, nine days after the birth of her daughter, Theodora. In 1665, as the birth of her eighth child approached Alice Thornton thought of 'the pangs of childbearing, often remembering of that sad estate I was to pass and dangerous perils my soul was to find, even to the gates of death' (Joceline 1624; Jackson 1873). Aristocratic and gentry women who married young ran an increased risk of death in childbirth, because they could expect to have more than the average number of pregnancies. This was not only because they had more procreative years ahead of them, but also because wealthier women eschewed nursing their own children and employed a wet-nurse instead.

The use of wet-nurses was contrary to the advice of conduct book writers, such as William Gouge, who advised that breastfeeding was a godly maternal duty, which would forge greater love between parents and child. Women who breastfed their children had longer intervals between births, perhaps by as much as a year, than those who did not (McLaren 1985). This may be because lactation acts as a restraint on fertility, but it also reflects the medical opinion of the day which advised that a lactating woman should not have intercourse because it would make her milk unwholesome. How far this advice was followed is impossible to say, but for the landed classes the continuation of the male line was all-important and breastfeeding was regarded as a hindrance to the getting of male heirs.

In general the babies of relatively wealthy parents, or abandoned or orphaned children, were wet-nursed. The nurses were generally chosen with care and were well-paid, and Valerie Fildes has found no evidence that they systematically ill-treated their charges or that the mortality rate was significantly higher amongst children raised in this fashion. The normal practice was to send the child to the home of the nurse, especially if the parents lived in a town, as it was believed that country air would be beneficial to the infant's health. Some richer families employed a wet-nurse in the household, where she could be supervised more closely by the mother (Fildes 1988). This was the practice followed by Lady Brilliana Harley and one of her letters from 1626 gives us an insight into how weaning was managed. Lady Harley described how her elder son Ned, who was eighteen months old, was kept away from the nurse, who was now caring for the newborn son: 'Ned has taken his weaning well, but is not admitted to see his nurse. Mary Wood has the charge of him, and it is all I require of her that she do that well. He lies in the nursery' (BL Add. MSS, 70001 fo. 204^r).

There are isolated references to the use of sponges or condoms in the second half of the seventeenth century, but most couples who wished to restrict family size probably used *coitus interruptus*. The use of abortifacients was condemned by the courts but knowledge about them was widespread and printed herbals were full of recipes to encourage regular menstruation, many of which were powerful enough to have resulted in miscarriage. Pregnant women were frequently advised not to make use of herbs which had this effect such as rue and savin and there is evidence that this knowledge was used to terminate unwanted pregnancies (Eccles 1982; Pollock 1990). If the pregnancy was at an early stage such an act was easier to conceal, but once the baby was felt to move, or quicken, then more blame was attached to any attempt to abort it. In 1578 Mercy Gold, a servant under suspicion of disposing of the body of a newborn child, claimed that her mistress, Elizabeth Bowyer, had given her a 'cruel, hot drink ... which provoked me often times to be delivered of my child'. After local gossip confirmed that the child had been secretly buried a group of eight women headed by the local midwife, Denis[e] Clark, had confronted Mercy and extracted a confession from her (PRO SP/12/ 130/52).

The delivery of a child was normally marked by the ceremony of churching when the mother was joined in church by her midwife or other women who had attended the birth, her gossips. Childbirth was a life event which was overwhelmingly dominated by women's concerns and the rituals attendant on it provide evidence of female networks of support and obligation. Before the Reformation, churching had been described in church liturgies as the purification of women after childbirth and it marked the return of the mother to society after her period of lying-in. It also coincided with the time when women were popularly thought to be physically fit enough to resume sexual relations with their husbands. In the 1552 Prayer Book the ceremony was described as 'the thanksgiving of women after childbirth commonly called the churching of women'. Neverthless it later aroused opposition from puritans, who regarded it as a superstitious

Catholic ritual which implied that women were unclean after child-birth.

Some puritan women actively refused to be churched and were articulate in their refusal to the Church authorities. In 1603 the wife of Thomas Starr of Ashford declared before the Church court that 'her conscience would not suffer her to do so, because she never read in the scriptures of any such kind of churching in women'(CCA X4/5 fo. 161^v). Although some historians have argued that churching was unpopular and that most women merely submitted to the practice, it would be wrong to assume that all women held the views expressed by Mrs Starr. Cressy concludes that most women were unconcerned with these theological points and actively enjoyed the occasion as part of a distinctively female rite of passage (Cressy 1997). Churching was a celebration of the mother's survival of the dangers of childbirth and women were churched even if their baby was stillborn or had died in the first weeks of infancy. In these cases the public support of female helpers may have been all the more crucial to the mourning mother.

Despite the large number of children that a woman might have, the death of a child or other family member was undoubtedly a matter of intense grief. In her *Memoirs* Lady Ann Fanshawe recorded the death of her daughter Ann at the age of nine in 1654, which made both her parents 'wish to go into the grave with her'. Katherine Clarke wrote of the death of her youngest child that 'it lay very heavy upon my spirit ... I lay long under the burden of that loss'. Alice Thornton felt that the death of her five-month-old daughter was a divine punishment and she reacted to the news that her husband was ill in 1668 'with excessive grief and fears upon me for his life and safety'. His death was a terrible loss to her 'in being deprived of my sweet and exceeding dear husband's life' (Loftis 1979; Clarke 1677; Jackson 1873).

Despite the exhortations of male writers that most women should marry and obey their husbands, the experience of family life was considerably more varied. A minority of women throughout the period did not marry at all, or delayed marriage while they amassed sufficient resources, and many women conducted sexual relationships outside the bounds of marriage altogether. The growth of female literacy and the greater survival of personal documentation make it possible to illustrate women's perceptions of family life from their own writing with increasing ease by the late seventeenth century, among the educated elite at any rate. Private and institutional papers also provide evidence of the ways in which women exercised authority within

Weald College Learning Centre
Brookshill, Harrow Weald, Mxldx.
HA3 6RR   0181 420 8846

family and community networks. Women made claims to particular authority in relation to childbirth, but they also acted as marriage brokers for younger relatives, as active agents in choosing their own husbands or lovers and as advisers to their husbands. Such activities reveal some of the disparities between the exhortations of the conduct books and an individual's reponses to the practical problems of being a daughter, sister, wife or mother.

CHAPTER EIGHT

Work

The first major scholarly investigation of women's work in the early modern period was Alice Clark's *Working life of women in the seventeenth century* (1919), which was influenced by socialist theories about the effects of the growth of capitalism and the Industrial Revolution. Clark divided economic production into three different systems: domestic industry, in which goods were produced solely for the use of the family and were not subject to exchange or money value; family industry, in which the family was the unit of production of goods for sale or exchange; and capitalistic industry or industrialism, in which production was controlled by the owners of capital and their labourers received wages.

Clark argued that the first two systems existed side by side in the middle ages when women's work was highly valued. The third system developed from the thirteenth century onwards, but made particularly rapid advances in the seventeenth century when work was taken out of the home and concentrated in separate workplaces. Under this system, women of the wealthier classes retreated into 'idleness and pleasure' while the wives of craftsmen could no longer help their husbands, and were forced to become unpaid domestic servants in their own homes or to seek separate employment of their own. In agriculture there was an expansion of waged labour for men but employment opportunities for women were reduced.

Clark's work provided an important starting point for the investigation of the economic status of women in the early modern period, but it has now been widely challenged. Judith Bennett has argued that women's work had always been low status and low paid and there was no golden age of equality which was destroyed by capitalism and the Industrial Revolution. It is also the case that variations in local economies and between different trades and industries were also far more important than Clark realized (Clark 1992; Bennett 1988; Vickery 1993).

The analysis of the status of women's work must also take into account the economy of England as a whole. The drastic and sustained fall in population after the first outbreaks of the Black Death in the mid-fourteenth century created economic opportunities for women, but when the population began to increase again towards the end of the fifteenth century these began to contract. In London there is evidence from the late middle ages that girls were apprenticed to certain trades, but the population rise in the sixteenth century led to a surplus of labour and girls were then edged out of the crafts by male apprentices. There was a decline in women's participation in certain areas of the London economy from 1480, which Kay Lacey has suggested may be related to growing attempts by the guilds and livery companies to exclude *feme sole* traders from certain occupations (Goldberg 1992; Barron 1989; Lacey 1985).

Similar changes have been detected elsewhere, but after 1640 the situation changed as the effects of warfare and a drop in population numbers may have worked to the benefit of female employment. The English population almost doubled between 1541, when it stood at about 2.77 million, and the mid-1650s, when it peaked at about 5.25 million. As a consequence there was inflation in the price of certain goods, although cash wages failed to keep pace with the increases. Staple foodstuffs were most affected by the price rises: the cost of grain, for example, rose approximately five-fold between the early sixteenth century and the mid-seventeenth century. The rate of population growth began to slow in the first half of the seventeenth century and from the late 1650s the population fell until it reached 4.86 million in 1686, and then began to increase once again. It has been suggested that the drop in the rate of population growth was a response to the earlier rapid price rises. As a result couples delayed marriage to avoid the cost of setting up independent households. The drop in population was also caused by emigration and by deaths in the Civil Wars. Approximately 540,000 people, the majority of them men, emigrated to the New World, Ireland and the Continent between 1630 and 1700 (Wrigley & Schofield 1989; Coleman 1977; Cressy 1987).

It has also been estimated that there were nearly 85,000 combat fatalities between 1642 and 1651 and that roughly 100,000 soldiers and civilians died in England from war-related diseases. This does not include the numbers of English soldiers killed fighting in Scotland and Ireland between the late 1630s and the mid-1650s. Wrigley and Schofield note that fertility fell sharply between 1646 and 1651 and consider whether defective registration of baptisms could be responsible. They conclude that this was not the case and suggest instead that the dip in gross reproduction rates between 1650 and 1681 was in part an indirect result of the sexual imbalance in emigration. They do not consider the fact that deaths in battle were at their highest between 1643 and 1645 and that the years from 1646 to 1651 coincided with the period when the greatest numbers of English troops were sent to Ireland. By 1652, when Ireland had been conquered by Cromwell, there were approximately 33,000 parliamentarian soldiers there, only a third of whom settled permanently (Carlton 1992; Gentles 1992). The effect of the Civil Wars on demographic change, and on female employment and marriage prospects still requires extensive research.

By far the largest source of employment was agriculture which was subject to considerable regional variations. The highland zone in the north and west of the country was characterized by sheep and cattle farming, while the lowland zone to the east and south was an area of largely arable farming, although these divisions were not rigid. These zones could be further divided into more distinct regions consisting of wolds and downlands, arable and pastoral vales, marshlands, heathlands, forests, fells, moorland and fenlands. They contained a range of landholdings from the large country estates of the aristocracy and gentry to substantial farms and smallholdings, some of which were insufficient to support a family. Smallholders and landless labourers were most likely to turn to additional work or by-employment to earn a living.

The most important industrial enterprise was the production of woollen cloth for the home and export markets. The textile industry was expanding rapidly in the late fifteenth century and the first half of the sixteenth century, but it then encountered vigorous competition from continental producers of lighter cloths and became subject to slumps and stagnation. The influx of religious refugees from the Netherlands and France, from the 1560s onwards, helped to encourage the production of the 'new draperies' in England and to open new markets in the Mediterranean for these cloths. The manufacture of cloth was labour intensive and was concentrated in the market towns and villages of the West Country, East Anglia, the West Riding of Yorkshire and the Weald of Kent, all areas where there was a surplus

of labour. There were independent weavers, but the cloth was produced largely by the putting-out system, which allowed the wool producers to pay for the wool to be carded and spun, and the cloth to be
woven, by workers in their own homes. Only the fulling, dyeing and
sometimes finishing needed to be completed outside the domestic
setting (Holderness 1976; Coleman 1977).

The period also witnessed the growth of a number of urban centres,
including London, the population of which increased from about
120,000 in 1550 to about 375,000 by 1650. It has been estimated that in
the 1520s 5.5 per cent of the population lived in towns of more than
5,000 inhabitants, and that this proportion had grown to 13.5 per cent
by 1670. Much of the increase came from migration and in the last
decades of the seventeenth century women migrants were in the
majority. Towns offered women opportunities to find work largely as
servants or in trade, but they also harboured concentrations of impo-
verished women. Censuses of the poor show a considerable imbalance
between the sexes; for example, in 1587 in Warwick and in 1625 in
Salisbury, two-thirds of the adult poor were women. Diane Willen has
argued that this reflects the social policy of the age which saw women,
children and the elderly as deserving poor, while able-bodied men
were more likely to be penalized as idle (Dyer 1991; Wrigley 1986;
Souden 1984; Willen 1988). While Willen's explanation goes some way
to explaining the 'feminization' of the poor, this phenomenon was also
caused by the lower rates of pay offered to women and by the effects of
life-cycle employment, which restricted their work opportunities if
they had young children.

The attempt to trace women's roles throughout these economic
developments is complicated by the fact that they are often under-
represented in the sources. Women rarely appear as householders and
the occupations of married women are frequently not documented. In
their study of the Essex village of Terling between 1525 and 1700
Wrightson and Levine found specific occupational designations for
400 villagers below the rank of gentleman, but the occupations of
women were rarely given. The few that appeared were servants, alehouse keepers or midwives. They concluded that women were engaged
mostly in domestic work or unspecialized agricultural labour
(Wrightson and Levine 1979). Work for the majority of men and
women was directly connected to their age. Before marriage women
might work as servants, which would allow them to accumulate some
capital towards a dowry. After marriage women in rural areas were

mainly concerned with domestic and farm labour, and perhaps some by-employment.

Women were particularly associated with brewing, dairying and spinning. Female predominance in the dairy trade continued into the late nineteenth century and there is also evidence that women outnumbered men in the manufacture of textiles, where they usually took the less skilled and less well paid jobs. Women were to experience a considerable loss of work and income as a result of mechanization of the textile industry in the late eighteenth century (Kussmaul 1981; Middleton 1985). In urban areas women worked particularly in the petty retail trades such as the production of food and drink and in service industries as servants, laundresses and nurses. Women were also regarded as having specific medical skills, such as the ability to make simple medicines from herbs, although in the seventeenth century male practitioners increasingly decried their lack of knowledge and training.

The authors of printed manuals of husbandry and advice books assumed that there would be a division of labour between husband and wife. John Fitzherbert in *The book of husbandry* (1534) wrote that it was the wife's occupation 'to winnow all manner of corns, to make malt, to wash and wring, to make hay, shear corn'. On the land the more physically demanding tasks such as ploughing and mowing with the scythe were regarded as men's work, but Fitzherbert also noted that in time of need the wife should help her husband to 'fill the dung cart, drive the plough, to load hay, corn and such other', which was probably a closer reflection of actual practice for the less wealthy. It also fell to the wife to go to the market to sell 'butter, cheese, milk, eggs, chickens, capons, hens, pigs, geese and all manner of corns'. Gervase Markham, the author of one of the most popular domestic manuals, *The English housewife* (1615), set out advice specifically for women on medicine, cookery, distillation, wine, dyeing and spinning wool, dairying, making malt, the use of oats, brewing and baking.

The theoretical differentiation between men and women's work was reflected in the lower wage rates set for women in various occupations. A royal proclamation of 1595 setting out wages in Exeter stipulated that during the hay harvest men were to be paid 3d a day with meat and drink, and 6d without. A woman was to receive 2d with meat and drink, and 4d without. Male servants aged between 16 and 20 were to receive no more than 20s a year. From the age of 20 to 24 years this rose to no more than 26s 8d and a livery, or 5s in lieu of livery.

Unmarried female servants between 16 and 24 were allowed no more than 16s a year and 5s for clothing. Female servants aged 24 years upwards were allowed no more than 20s for wages and 6s 8d for clothes. The figures for servants reflect the fact that they would be living with their masters and would receive bed and board. Rates set by the justices of the peace for Herefordshire in 1632 reflect the same assumptions that women should receive lower wages. Mowers and reapers were to receive 12d a day without refreshment, and 6d a day with meat and drink. A female reaper received 8d and 4d respectively. A maidservant was to receive 20s per annum, but a dairymaid received 96s 8d reflecting the greater skill required of her (Hughes & Larkin 1964; HMC). Even if these wage rates were not rigidly observed, they do show the expectation that women could only command lower wages than men.

In his study of Wiltshire, Underdown has argued that there were considerable differences in the employment of women in different agricultural areas. Pastoral regions, he suggests, were traditionally areas of high female employment and the growth of the economy in these areas of Wiltshire gave women there more financial independence. The market economy was expanding in the county in the sixteenth century and more land was devoted to dairying, giving more women access to a lucrative trade. Women were also involved in the local clothmaking industry as spinners. The wood–pasture regions where they worked were typified by individually owned enclosed farms and relatively large parishes with scattered populations. There was consequently less social control there than in arable areas, with characteristically smaller parishes and nucleated village centres, often with resident gentry and stronger manorial institutions.

Underdown has argued that in areas where social control was weak and more women were economically independent, including towns, there is evidence of strained relations between men and women. The wood–pasture regions, for example, resorted more frequently than arable areas to public shaming rituals, known as charivari or skimmingtons, in order to control women who were regarded as scolds or had otherwise contravened patriarchal authority. According to Underdown prosecutions of women for scolding were also higher in the towns and the wood–pasture regions of the county. He links this to the increase in witchcraft prosecutions and the circulation of printed literature attacking women to argue that there was a general 'gender crisis' in England between 1560 and 1640 as men struggled to retain patriarchal control over women. Ingram has, however, cast doubt on the idea that there was a marked rise in scolding cases after 1560 since prosecutions for scolding were commonplace in some courts between the late fourteenth century and the early sixteenth century (Under-down 1985; Ingram 1994). A further problem with this analysis lies in the fact that overtly misogynistic literature was not a new phenom-enon and its popular roots lay firmly in the middle ages. The increased number of anti-women texts published from the early 1580s onwards may simply reflect the expansion in print culture as books became cheaper and more titles covering a variety of subjects were produced to satisfy an increasingly literate audience.

Part of Underdown's argument rests on evidence taken from towns, and as we have seen the urban population was a minority reaching no more than 15 per cent by the end of the period. There is thus a further danger of transferring concerns from the urban environment to the general population. Urban records can, however, be used to uncover patterns of female work. Guild records show that women learned various trades and crafts or ran their own businesses, but they rarely represented more than a small minority of apprentices or guild members. Moreover, women rarely acted as town officials or took part in the process of town government.

Under common law a woman who was single or widowed could legally carry on a trade as a *feme sole*. A married women, as a *feme covert*, could not own property or make contracts, rendering it tech-nically impossible to own a business in her own right except in certain towns, where borough custom allowed wives to own property for the purposes of trade if the husband agreed. In London a number of married women traded as *feme soles* and Caroline Barron suggests this practice may have gone back to the early thirteenth century. It sur-vived in London until the nineteenth century, after it had died out elsewhere. Peter Earle has noted that in the late seventeenth and early eighteenth century few girls in London were apprenticed to trades and they were to be found in a few 'feminine' occupations such as millin-ery, mantua-making, lace-making, branches of the silk industry and some shopkeeping trades. None of these was likely to lead to a great accumulation of capital or stock. Earle also noted that the wives of rich citizens were withdrawing from trade and were opting for an 'idle and frivolous' life (Barron 1989; Earle 1989).

In Oxford a number of wives were trading in the middle ages, but according to Mary Prior between 1500 and 1800 no such cases were documented. In Oxford widows were not allowed to become freemen, but they could take over their husbands' businesses if they paid quarterage to his guild and observed its regulations. Widows who continued to trade in this way can be traced through the enrolment of apprentices and this reveals a small number of active female traders up to 1700. They were however never more than five per cent of the total number taking on apprentices. Prior found that when the town's economy was expanding after 1560 there was a lower incidence of widows carrying on a husband's trade, but when the economy was stagnant in the late seventeenth century (between 1671 and 1700) the figures rose. In a study of Bristol, Ben-Amos has found that out of 1,500 private apprentices enrolled in the town between 1542 and 1552 only 3.3 per cent were female. These figures remained low into the seventeenth century when a sample of 1,945 private and parish apprentices bound between 1600 and 1645 shows that 2.2 per cent were female.

Female apprenticeships in the town were distinct from those of the males as very few of the girls were apprenticed to a craft. In Ben-Amos's sample taken from the sixteenth century two-thirds of the girls were apprenticed as housewives or sempstresses. A fifth were bound to a trade as drapers, grocers, vintners and a mercer, and only a few were bound to craftsmen as joiners, pinners, cofferers and a bell-founder. Ben-Amos found that by the early seventeenth century the pattern of female apprenticeship had changed. Girls were then usually bound as servants or in the clothing industry where they were trained for the lower paid jobs. Ben-Amos argues that entry into urban crafts was becoming more competitive in the early Stuart period. Apprenticeships for girls were thus contracting as the population increased and women were pushed out of the retail trades and crafts where they had earlier gained limited entry (Prior 1985; Ben-Amos 1994).

The Bristol records also show widows trading on their own account in the seventeenth century, which Ben-Amos argues demonstrates there were opportunities for them to learn crafts and trades outside the formal apprenticeship system. The occupational distribution of widows did not differ significantly from that of male craftsmen and traders, and they included ironmongers, shoemakers, leatherworkers and retailers. It is most likely that they learned these trades from their fathers or husbands. In Bristol women could be made free, but as with Oxford the number of widows who were members of guilds was low and they represented less than four per cent of the total membership in the first half of the seventeenth century.

Sue Wright has pointed out in the case of Salisbury that many female occupations were not regulated by the guilds, and women were principally employed at the 'casual, menial end of the market'. Salisbury was badly affected by the slump in the cloth trade from the mid-sixteenth century and was particularly badly hit in the 1620s. Wright concurs with the general thesis that women had better job opportunities when trade was good for the town as a whole. Women in the town were particularly involved in spinning, lacemaking, knitting and buttonmaking, all occupations that were traditionally associated with the poor. Wright also found evidence of Salisbury women acting as alehouse keepers and, on a small scale, as pawnbrokers and money-lenders (Wright 1985).

Women could also be directly employed by town corporations or other urban institutions. Norwich, for example, operated one of the most advanced poor relief systems in the Elizabethan period. In the 1570s and 1580s the town employed women to teach up to twelve pauper children in their own homes and in 1630 the city decreed that 'a knitting schooldame' should be appointed in every parish to set children and the poor on work. After the Reformation women also helped to staff the city's seven or so hospitals and the lazar houses, where the sick, the elderly and the mentally ill were looked after. They also acted as keepers for institutions housing paupers in the city. Similar initiatives can be found in towns such as York, London and Salisbury. The nursing skills of women were particularly apparent during outbreaks of plague and in the Elizabethan period women were employed in the London parishes to view the sick for signs of plague. In Ipswich in 1579 women were paid a shilling a day to attend houses visited by the plague and they also viewed and prepared dead bodies for burial (Willen 1988).

Women performed other services that were more specifically associated with their sex, such as prostitution, wet-nursing or midwifery, although men-midwives were practising in small numbers from the early seventeenth century. In towns such as London or York certain areas were notorious as the centres of bawdy houses, but prostitution was not solely an urban phenomenon. In rural areas it was associated with tippling houses, often run by women, and some prostitutes were migrants who travelled from parish to parish in search of custom. The Church courts could prosecute prostitutes for fornication and in 1546

Henry VIII issued a proclamation closing down the London brothels, the effects of which soon lapsed. There was, however, little systematic attempt to regulate the trade or to close the brothels permanently except during the revolutionary years of the 1640s and 1650s (Quaife 1979; Hughes & Larkin 1964; Durston 1989).

Wet-nurses were employed by the wealthier and for babies whose mothers had died or abandoned them. The overall numbers and distribution of wet-nurses are still matters for further research, but initial investigation undertaken by Dorothy McLaren indicates that parishes in the home counties around London probably had a high concentration of wet-nurses who looked after children from the city. Wet-nursing was relatively well paid and amounted to a form of by-employment in these areas (McLaren 1985). More is known about the activities of midwives, who operated both in towns and rural areas. They were licensed by the Church of England, except during the civil war period when the Church court system broke down. It is clear, however, that throughout the period many women worked as midwives without ever obtaining the necessary licence, either because of the cost or because they were not members of the established Church.

Some women acted very informally and helped at the childbed of friends and neighbours without any payment. Others accepted payment, but pursued midwifery as a by-employment, and some had an extensive clientele. Professional midwives were often married to clerics, physicians or lawyers. Training for midwives consisted mainly of practical experience, both as mothers themselves and as attendants at the deliveries of other women. There were also a number of printed manuals of midwifery, the earliest of which was *The birth of mankind* (1540) translated from German, although it was not until 1671 that a midwife published a manual reflecting her own practices when Jane Sharp wrote *The midwives book*.

A number of unsuccessful attempts were made to organize midwives into a professional body in the seventeenth century. The first of these occurred in 1616 when a group of London midwives petitioned King James for the incorporation of a company of midwives to train and license them. This was resisted by the Royal College of Physicians on the grounds that it was neither necessary nor convenient and 'a thing not exampled in any commonwealth'. One of the few early male midwives, Peter Chamberlain, also attempted to create a company of midwives in London in 1634, but he was then opposed by women, who feared he would take over their profession, although in fact man-midwives were quite rare until the 1720s.

In 1687 the midwife Elizabeth Cellier outlined her plan for the foundation of a Royal Hospital as a college for midwives. Although she claimed to have the backing of James II the plan was not realized, perhaps because of her own rather doubtful political background as a Catholic intriguer. In a series of pamphlets her political opponents made much of her religion and her profession and smeared her with the charge that all midwives were drunk and ignorant. These and other attacks on the profession by male writers blackened the reputation of midwives and even in 1977 Lawrence Stone observed that midwives were 'ignorant and ill-trained', a conclusion that is not borne out by the evidence provided by early modern women themselves. Midwives were also erroneously believed by historians to be more likely than other women to be accused of witchcraft. The research of David Harley has refuted this last myth and recent research into the practice of midwives has revealed that they were in general highly regarded by their clients (Eccles 1982; Beier 1987; Wilson 1995; Stone 1977; Harley 1990).

Some midwives built up considerable expertise and lucrative businesses. The survival of an anonymous London midwife's journal covering the years 1694 to 1723 shows that during this period she made 676 deliveries. Testimonials for midwives seeking licences in the post-1660 period also testify to their competence and to the fact that they could expect repeat business from satisfied mothers. If midwives were generally well regarded by the mothers they delivered, their expertise was also recognized in other areas. They and other matrons (respectable married women with children), were employed, for example, in witchcraft cases to search the bodies of the accused for evidence of the witch's mark. They were also brought in to decide whether a woman was pregnant, in cases where she pleaded 'the belly' in order to escape capital punishment, or if a widow was pregnant by her late husband, which could affect the inheritance of an estate.

In cases of infanticide, midwives and other women would be asked whether in their opinion the accused had recently given birth. They might also find themselves asked to judge male potency or female virginity when wives sought to annul their marriage on the grounds of non-consummation. The most notorious case in which this occurred was the divorce of Frances Howard from the Earl of Essex when two midwives and four matrons were selected to examine the countess and they concluded that she was a virgin without any physical deformity that would render copulation impossible (Evenden 1993; Oldham 1985; Lindley 1993).

The decline of the midwife was an eighteenth century phenomenon which occurred as male physicians and *accoucheurs* were able to offer more fashionable medical interventions into the process of birth. Such a development might be taken as part-confirmation of Alice Clark's general thesis that opportunities for women's work were being eroded from the seventeenth century. As has been argued in this chapter, however, the economic position of women was always inferior to that of men. Women's wages were generally lower than men's and this, combined with increasing competition for employment, contributed to a distinct 'feminization' of poverty in the sixteenth century if not earlier. Some pursuits certainly offered women potentially lucrative occupations such as dairying, wet-nursing and midwifery, but the majority of women on the land were involved in farming in some capacity, and in towns they were involved primarily in retail and service industries. These were prone to economic fluctuation over time and from region to region and they do not conform to Alice Clark's model of linear decline across the seventeenth century. It is perhaps too early to state with any certainty what the overall effects of these developments on women might have been, but some initial observations can be made.

Medieval historians have indicated that after the initial outbreaks of the Black Death women were able to exploit the economic gaps created by the fall in population. Increasingly, however, economic restrictions were placed on women, particularly in towns, between the late fifteenth century and the mid-seventeenth century. These were the results of a growing population and surplus labour force, which meant that there was more competition amongst men for the available work. Consequently, as Prior and Ben-Amos have both argued, women were disadvantaged in the early Tudor and the early Stuart period. In the late seventeenth century Prior has detected greater activity amongst widows as trade in Oxford stagnated. This coincided with a drop in the general population and opportunities may have opened for women as a result. Trade in Oxford, which was the royalist headquarters in the 1640s, may also have suffered from the long-term effects of the deaths of adult males in the Civil Wars, although this possibility is not explored by Prior. How far this also affected the economic position of women elsewhere still awaits detailed investigation. Similarly, more regional studies of women's work and wealth in both towns and agrarian areas are needed before definite conclusions about long-term economic trends can be drawn.

CHAPTER NINE

Religion

Throughout the period 1500-1700 the functions of the priesthood, which involved preaching and the administration of the sacraments, were regarded almost exclusively as male preserves. This led the clergy, in particular, to emphasize the divisions between the public sphere as a male arena and the private sphere as a women's arena. The religious strictures placed on women were justified particularly through reference to the New Testament writings of St Paul, a key example being his injunctions to the Corinthians, which in Tyndale's influential revised translation of 1534 read 'let your wives keep silence in the congregations. For it is not permitted unto them to speak: but let them be under obedience, as saith the law. If they will learn anything, let them ask their husbands at home' (1 Corinthians, 14).

Nevertheless, religious belief provided women with some measure of public influence and a way in which their personal authority within their household and community might be enhanced. Indeed contemporaries believed that women were more inclined to piety than men and this was accepted as a legitimate justification for some actions. Female adherents were active, for example, amongst the Lollards, who criticized the established Catholic church from the 1380s and were gradually absorbed into the Protestant movement from the 1520s onwards. Women were similarly involved in underground Protestant circles in the reigns of Henry VIII and Mary Tudor. Female adherents later helped Catholicism to survive as a substantial minority religion after the Elizabethan Settlement of 1559 had outlawed the old faith.

These persecuted religious minorities, and the later puritan sects which sprang up from the 1560s, provided much greater religious freedom for the laity than the established Church could. They lacked strict hierarchies and both men and women were able to make varied contributions to their development. This is particularly well documented amongst the civil war sects in the 1640s and 1650s. Richard Coppin wrote in 1659 that in any assembly a woman had the 'freedom to speak and answer as a man' and the Quaker leader, George Fox, argued that the spirit of Christ may 'speak in the female as well as the male', but their ideas remained the hallmark of religious radicalism and were not adopted by more orthodox thinkers (Cross 1978; Thomas 1958; Laurence 1990; Trevett 1991; Durston 1989).

Women also clearly played an important role in preserving and transmitting religious belief from one generation to the next. Their involvement in maintaining religious traditions within their families also explains, in part, the geographical concentration of certain groups, such as the Lollards in the midlands and the south of England, or later the recusant Catholics in northern and south-western England and along the English/Welsh border country. The involvement of women in these minority groups was made much of by hostile contemporaries, who exaggerated the licence given to women as a way of discrediting unorthodox religious movements. Often, however, it is through these hostile accounts that we can uncover evidence about individual women's activities and the debates that they generated.

There is evidence from the fifteenth century that Lollard women were encouraged to teach religious precepts and this could involve preaching. The early Lollards even discussed the possibility of women administering the sacrament of communion, although it is doubtful that they ever did so. This last argument was based on the fact that midwives and mothers could baptize babies in the absence of a priest if the child's life was in danger. In her history of women and religion from 1500 to 1720 Crawford has emphasized that the apparent greater religiosity of women was not a natural difference between men and women; it was a social construct and some women successfully used it to contest the restrictions of early modern patriarchy (Eales 1992; Rowlands 1985; Aston 1980; McSheffrey 1995; Crawford 1993).

One of the major problems in studying the religious beliefs of people in the early modern period lies in the fact that dissenters are often better documented than conformists. We should not overlook the fact that evidence contained in the official documents of the pre-Reformation Catholic Church, such as wills and churchwardens' accounts, indicates that laywomen were widely involved in the official religious culture of the late middle ages. They raised money for their parish churches, left bequests to the fabric of the church, and occasionally acted as churchwardens. Wealthier women acted as patronesses, commissioning the writing of saints' lives or the making of images or other religious art, and leaving endowments to religious institutions.

Certain saints such as the Virgin Mary, St Anne and St Margaret of Antioch were particularly associated with the female culture of pregnancy and childbirth and were especially venerated by women. The cult of saints was further encouraged amongst female parishioners by the pre-Reformation form of churching, which involved the lighting of a candle in thanksgiving at the image of the Virgin or at the Lady altar in the parish church. Many women, such as Cecile Messenger, who left a cloth for the altar of Saint Anne in 1528 to the church at Tonge, Kent, demonstrated a particular devotion to such female saints. When the Henrician Reformation gradually removed the veneration of saints some women were prepared to resort to extreme measures in their defence. At Exeter a group of women armed themselves with spikes, shovels and other tools to defend the images of St Nicholas's Priory from destruction. After chasing a workman from the church, Elizabeth Glandfield assaulted an alderman who tried to pacify them. They then staged a sit-in which only ended when the mayor ordered the women's arrest. Such was the ferocity of the women that rumours were flying that the group were in fact men disguised in women's clothing (Haigh 1993; Gibson 1990; Duffy 1990; Hussey 1907; Youings 1971).

Before the Reformation a variety of occupations allowed some women to pursue a life that was openly dedicated to religious piety, while also maintaining interaction with and influence over their local communities. The most well-documented and researched of these is the life of the nun, but many laywomen also lived communal lives bounded by religious duties in hospitals, where they tended for or prayed for the poor, the sick and the elderly. At the Reformation there were approximately 800 hospitals in England and most of them contained mixed communities of men and women. Some women also lived more informally in private houses, sometimes termed *maisons dieu*, where they undertook voluntary poverty and dispensed charity in imitation of the continental beguine movement. In her innovative archaeological study of religious women in the middle ages, Roberta Gilchrist has suggested that the number of women living in this way may have been seriously underestimated by historians of medieval piety (Gilchrist 1994).

Hospitals and *maisons dieu* were largely to be found in towns and mainly recruited women of the urban and lower social classes. In contrast nunneries were more commonly in rural areas and the conventual life supported a small number of women who were drawn mainly from noble and gentry families. In general it was only wealthier families who could afford the donations or dowries expected on entry to the convents and, as Eileen Power has pointed out, families lower down the social scale needed the labour of their womenfolk in agriculture and industry. Power estimated that when numbers were at their greatest in the mid-fourteenth century there were no more than 3,500 nuns in England and that this figure fell to about 1,900 in 1534 when there were some 142 nunneries in existence. Between then and 1540 the nunneries and monasteries were gradually closed by the reforming policies of Henry VIII's government. In 1540 the number of nuns who were dispossessed was approximately 1,600 (Power 1975, 1922; Knowles & Hadcock 1971).

Sixteenth-century Protestant propagandists and later historians alike have attributed the decline in numbers of nuns from the fourteenth century onwards to the somewhat nebulous and unquantifiable concept of growing 'corruption' in the Catholic Church. Yet the impact of demographic and economic factors should not be overlooked. The increased mortality rates which followed the first great outbreak of plague in the late 1340s resulted in a dramatic contraction of the population and continued to restrain population growth until the early sixteenth century. The population of England in 1541 was possibly only half of what it had been two centuries earlier (Wrigley and Schofield 1989). Thus from the second half of the fourteenth century onwards there was less economic pressure on families to place unmarried daughters in religious institutions. At the same time the endowments and incomes of the religious houses, both monasteries and nunneries, were falling in real terms and most religious houses could not afford to support the numbers of inmates that they had contained before the plague had first struck.

It is often impossible to discover whether a woman became a nun as a convenient alternative to marriage or because of the desire to pursue a religious vocation. Nevertheless, convents provided their inmates with a highly respected career which involved not only private observation of religious rules, but also a variety of public functions. Some nunneries ran educational establishments for girls, others were organized as hospitals, others were seen as sources of local charity and almsgiving, and most took female boarders as a means of supplementing their finances. Nuns were entrusted with the day to day running of their convent and controlled its income and property, and they also employed local people as servants and labourers. Although late medieval visitation records of the nunneries reveal incidents of slackness and incompetence, such evidence needs to be placed in context. Not all houses were sources of concern and individual nuns were regarded as living the most exemplary and holy lives. Shock stories of pregnant nuns being dismissed from their convents were exploited to the full at the Reformation but Claire Cross has found, for example, that – in early sixteenth-century Yorkshire – nunneries had no difficulty in recruiting novices and there was 'absolutely no evidence that young girls were turning away from the religious life' (Cross 1990).

Allied to the monastic ideal was the less common life of the recluse or anchorite, who lived in relative seclusion in order to pray and meditate. Ann Warren's study of anchorites in medieval England demonstrates that between the twelfth and sixteenth centuries the majority of anchorites were female, although the disparity was lessening by the early sixteenth century, when she identified 37 anchoresses, 27 male anchorites and 4 unknown (Warren 1985). Anchorites received financial support from their community in return for prayers. A succession of anchoresses living in the churchyard of St Mary's church in Faversham, Kent, for example, received several bequests in wills dated between 1471 and 1523 in return for prayers for the souls of the testators. The wills also reveal that there were female servants in attendance on the anchoresses (Hussey 1907).

The most famous English anchoress was Julian of Norwich whose mystical writings survive under the title *Revelations of divine love.* Julian was first recorded as living in a cell attached to a parish church in Norwich in 1400, where she was the recipient of numerous bequests, the last made in 1416. Her reputation as a religious adept was based on her role as a spiritual adviser to those who consulted her, amongst whom was the remarkable Margery Kempe, wife of a substantial burgess from King's Lynn, whose religious visions and pilgrimages were recorded in extraordinary detail in what has been described as 'the earliest surviving autobiographical writing in English' (Windeatt 1985).

Although the lives of Julian and Margery were unusual, they were tolerated by the established Church, because there was a tradition of acceptance of both male and female mystics. The later career of Elizabeth Barton, a visionary nun who was executed in 1534 for opposing the Henrician Reformation, is a revealing case of a woman whose religious revelations were initially accepted by the authorities, but who was subsequently denounced when her pronouncements became a political embarrassment. In 1525 at the age of about fifteen, Barton was working as a servant in a Kent village when she fell seriously ill and experienced the first of a series of visions of the Virgin Mary. She claimed to have received messages which endorsed Catholic doctrine and practices, and as news of this spread in the diocese of Canterbury she was investigated by a clerical commission under the direction of the archbishop, William Warham. At a time when early Lutheran books and ideas were circulating in Kent, Barton's orthodox defence of the mass, confession, invocation of the saints and the efficacy of good works was well received by the commission. She was persuaded to enter the nunnery of St Sepulchre's in Canterbury, where her visions continued and she became critical of Henry VIII's divorce and plans for religious reform. The death of Warham in late 1532 left Barton and her supporters in Canterbury dangerously exposed and she was attainted and executed along with two friars, two monks and a priest.

The public recantations of this group in Canterbury and in London along with their grisly public executions as traitors undoubtedly helped to publicize the dangers of opposition to the Henrician Reformation, at least in the south-east of England. The convent of St Sepulchre was suppressed in the following year and the prioress, Dame Philippa John, received the pension that was offered to all ex-religious and retired into private life. Unlike their male counterparts nuns could not find re-employment within the Church and at the Dissolution some nuns married, others continued to live in small communal groups and some joined convents abroad (Neame 1971; Rex 1991; Woodward 1966). From the late sixteenth century a number of religious communities were founded on the continent by English patrons and by 1642 at least 300 Englishwomen had joined these institutions. The most successful was the Institute of the Blessed Virgin Mary founded in 1616 by Mary Ward, which was initially unenclosed and was modelled on the Jesuit order (Rowlands 1985).

The death of Elizabeth Barton demonstrated that her piety was no safeguard against the hostility of the authorities. Women were, however, less likely than men to suffer the death penalty for their religious beliefs. This can be attributed perhaps to women's greater desire to conform, or more probably to the authorities' desire to show greater leniency to women, which is paralleled in the cases of other felonies at the time, apart from witchcraft and infanticide. Of the half dozen or so women burnt as heretics in Henry VIII's reign, the most well known was Anne Askew, who refused to accept the Catholic theology of transubstantiation and was executed in 1546. She wrote an account of her interrogation and torture, which was smuggled out of prison and printed by John Bale. It is a unique survival of the first-hand experiences of one of the female Protestant martyrs and, as Eve Beilin has demonstrated, played an important part in the longer-term redefinition of the role of women both within the Church and more generally in society (Beilin 1985).

Askew may well have provided a model for the martyrs who died in Mary Tudor's reign between 1555 and 1558. From a total of nearly 300, at least 55 of them were women, if we include those who died in prison awaiting trial or punishment. Their stories are recorded by the martyrologist John Foxe in his famous *Acts and monuments*, popularly known as the *Book of martyrs*, which rivalled the Bible in popularity and was first published in English in 1563. Foxe has been described as telling us 'more about the women of the Reformation in England than any other source' and he documented the stories of royal and noblewomen along with women of more obscure origins (Bainton 1975).

Thus Foxe records the martyrdom of Elizabeth Pepper, the wife of a weaver from Colchester, and Thomasine à Wood, a maid from Lewes, as well as chronicling the exile of Katherine, Duchess of Suffolk and the execution of Lady Jane Grey. Ellen Macek has argued that there is also strong evidence in Foxe's book that some of the martyrs participated in a female subculture which specifically offered support to women. Thus Foxe records that at Stoke, Suffolk, a group of women prayed for the conversion of a husband who tried to force his wife to conform to the Catholic faith. On her way to the stake in Lichfield a great number of Joyce Lewys's friends, especially the women of the town, symbolically offered their support by drinking from a cup with her. Foxe described the women martyrs as having 'a bold and manly stomach' that both enabled them to refute their persecutors and to face death with equanimity (Macek 1988).

At Mary Tudor's death in November 1558 the number of English men and women who were committed Protestants was a minority and they were largely concentrated in London, in other major towns such as Norwich and Bristol, and in the southern and eastern counties of

England. It took at least a generation for Protestantism to be seen as the securely established faith, a process that was coming to fruition by the 1580s. In the interim many of the laity continued to adhere to Catholic forms of religious expression and the ecclesiastical court records contain many instances of the laity defying the dictates of the new Protestant church. Traditional religious habits were deeply ingrained and women were especially unwilling to abandon some of the Catholic traditions associated with childbirth, such as prayers to the Virgin Mary or St Anne, which doubtless provided psychological support at a moment of physical pain and danger of death. Anxious enquiries by the Church authorities after 1559 indicate that Catholic midwives were still believed to be using religious relics such as supposed saints' belts to ease mothers' pains in childbed.

The Church court records reveal that many laity were slow to conform to the Protestant religion. In the first five or six years of Elizabeth's reign the records of the diocese of Canterbury, for example, reveal the activities of women such as Margery Inwood who continued to wear a rosary, of Widow Maisters, who kept a Catholic mass book and a banned religious image under her bedhead, of Mother Wells who derided the present religion and said she hoped they would shortly have mass again, and the wife of William Bell who left the parish church of Holy Cross Canterbury at the singing of psalms, 'cursing and railing' and used a Catholic book of prayers. The diocesan records throughout England tell a similar story (Willis 1975; Duffy 1990).

Marie Rowlands has pointed out that the resistance of Catholic women to the Protestant faith raised fundamental questions about the relationship between state power and the family. While unmarried women and widows could be prosecuted and fined by the church and secular authorities, doubt existed about whether a recusant wife was responsible for her actions and to what extent her husband should be punished if she did not conform. Catholic families took advantage of this and husbands attended church services regularly thus avoiding any confiscation of property or civil disability. Their wives often maintained Catholic worship and teaching within the household and attended the local parish church infrequently or not at all. In a study (cited by Rowlands) of 300 Catholic households in Yorkshire, Hugh Aveling discovered that two-thirds could be classified as matriarchal in that they were either headed by a widow, or the wife took the lead in maintaining Catholic allegiance. Surviving Catholic families were greatly aided in their resistance from the mid-1570s when English priests, who had trained in continental seminaries, began to return to England in increasing numbers to maintain the faith and to win converts. Networks of women played a vital role in sheltering and supporting the missionary priests in England and Wales. Three women, Margaret Clitherow, Margaret Ward and Anne Line were executed for harbouring priests, but other women successfully gave the priests food and shelter for brief periods from a few hours to a few days without discovery (Rowlands 1985).

There are some strong parallels between the experiences of Catholic women after the Elizabethan Settlement and the experiences of Protestant women during the earlier Marian persecution. These groups were both acting under the constraints of persecution when women of each religious persuasion were forced to take individual responsibility for defying the authorities on an unprecedented scale. On both sides the ability of women to assimilate religious teachings, to pass them on and even to use them in disputes against learned opponents was encouraged on a larger scale than ever before. In contrast, the position of conforming women after the Settlement might be interpreted as more submissive. Certainly such women had no need to confront the authorities and, without the Catholic option of the convent, their religious concerns were more likely to be focused on their households and families.

Nevertheless, religious faith still offered Protestant women the opportunity to take an active role in the promotion of spiritual values and in some cases to reinforce their personal authority at home and in the wider community. In trying to assess how far this was the case, historians are hampered by the fact that the contemporary evidence is dominated by nonconformists who drew the attention of the courts. Again the evidence of documents, such as wills and official accounts, shows that women were adopting Protestantism; but tracing the ways in which women internalized orthodox Protestant teachings and then utilized them in their everyday lives is not an easy task. For this we must turn to the evidence created by the most committed groups of Protestants, the puritans, many of whom were conformist, but operated on the radical edge of acceptable religious behaviour. Puritans saw themselves as a godly beleaguered minority battling against the indifference and sinfulness of those around them.

One of the most celebrated puritan documents is the diary of Lady Margaret Hoby, covering the period 1599-1605, which gives a broad insight into the day-to-day affairs of a conforming puritan gentlewoman. Lady Hoby lived in the East Yorkshire parish of Hackness, but travelled to both York and London to visit relatives or friends and to hear famous preachers. Her daily religious routine involved her in prayer, meditation, the examination of her conscience, reading and, although she had no children of her own, the instruction of other members of her household such as servants. It has been suggested by Keith Thomas that many women 'had more time for piety' than men (Meads 1930; Thomas 1958). Such an assumption could be made from a casual reading of the sources, but this would be a misguided interpretation, which confuses the ends with the means. Lady Hoby's diary and other similar documents, such as Lady Brilliana Harley's commonplace books, demonstrate the ways in which women actively used their religiosity to create conditions in which they could gain time away from the busy demands of family life (Eales 1990b). This time was spent in reading, writing or thinking about religion and was justified by the encouragement given to women to assimilate religious teachings and to pass them on to others.

Women could thus use their piety to assert what Peter Lake has called – in the case of Mrs Ratcliffe of Chester – 'personal potency' (Lake 1987). Funeral sermons and 'godly lives' contain some surprisingly personalized accounts of the ways in which women acted against all the expectations of conduct books. Katherine Brettergh, for example, the sister of the godly gentleman John Bruen of Cheshire, was described in 1606 as legitimately upbraiding her husband both for being angry on the Lord's day and for collecting rents from a tenant who was unable to pay, 'for then you oppress the poor', as she said. Richard Baxter's wife, Margaret, was active in collecting money for the puritan ministers who were ejected by the terms of the Act of Uniformity of 1662 and she openly criticized ministers who compromised their consciences on this issue. For this she was herself criticized by others for not being 'content to live privately and quietly' (Eales 1990b).

The most direct challenge to the authority of individual husbands came, however, from women who disagreed with their spouses about forms of religious worship. The question of whether a woman could defy her husband if he was ungodly arose as a practical problem during the early days of the Reformation when a number of women such as Anne Askew and Anne Locke separated from their Catholic husbands. Catholic priests later advised recusant wives to act in reli-

gious matters without their husband's consent or knowledge if necessary. Theologians and theoreticians generally argued that women
should obey their husbands unless their commands conflicted with
those of God (Collinson 1983; Rowlands 1985). The social dislocation
of the Civil Wars saw this doctrine pushed to its ultimate conclusion as
sectaries in particular began to explore the validity of divorce and
remarriage based on arguments of religious incompatibility (Thomas
1958; Durston 1989). Although there were examples of both men and
women deserting spouses and taking new ones for religious reasons in
this period, in practice this was not a new departure. As was stated in
Chapter Seven, informal separation and remarriage were not
unknown, but what was new was the justification of such behaviour
by reference to religious conscience.

Immediately before the outbreak of civil war, government control
over censorship began to break down and there was a rapid prolifera-
tion of discussion and publication about radical political, religious,
social and economic ideas. New independent religious groups sprang
up, which sought to exclude those who were seen as ungodly. That
women were attracted to these separatist groups in disproportionate
numbers in the 1640s and 1650s has already been noted. Such sects
afforded their female followers greater religious freedoms than the
established Church or the presbyterian system that replaced it after the
defeat in 1646 of Charles I in the First Civil War. There were, for
example, well documented cases from the early 1640s of women
preaching. There were also instances of female visionaries, whose
religious teachings took the form of mystical and prophetical pronouncements. Phyllis Mack has identified nearly 300 women who were
active as preachers, writers or evangelical missionaries in the years
from 1640 to 1665 (Hinds 1996; Mack 1992). Her list includes Anna
Trapnel, the Fifth Monarchist, who used her spoken and printed pro-
phecies to attack the Cromwellian regime in the 1650s, and Margaret
Fell, one of the founders of the Quaker movement, who advocated the
right of women to preach in her book *Women's speaking justified*
published in 1666.

Women were particularly active amongst the Quakers, perhaps
because the Friends did not have an ordained ministry, but held that
all believers could address religious meetings if the spirit moved them
to do so. Nevertheless, the involvement of women did meet some
resistance amongst the Friends and this was solved partially by the
institution of separate women's meetings from the late 1650s. These

meetings helped to create female networks dedicated to missionary work and to raising money for the families of imprisoned Friends. The prominence achieved by women within the Quaker movement at this time is reflected in the fact that in the years 1651-60 their writings amounted to nearly half of all publications by women, although this activity subsequently diminished sharply (Laurence 1990; Trevett 1991; Crawford 1985).

After the Restoration of the monarchy in 1660, the Quakers and other nonconformist groups such as the baptists, congregationalists and presbyterians all sought to distance themselves from the more radical religious and political ideas which had been circulating during the civil war years of the 1640s and under the republican government in the 1650s. The result was the severe curtailing of women's activities within these groups. In the long term the apparent freedoms afforded by the years of civil war and interregnum were not to be translated into permanent gains.

CHAPTER TEN

Crime and the courts

Women were prosecuted in the secular and Church courts for a variety of offences, but the sensational nature of witchcraft has led historians to focus heavily on this particular crime. Contemporary pamphlets and ballads reveal intense anxieties about witchcraft and other crimes associated with women, particularly the killing of children and husbands, which were seen as both unnatural and as disruptive of social order (Dolan 1994). The murder of a man by his wife, or by any other subordinate, was regarded a form of treason; and in *The country justice* (1615) the lawyer, Michael Dalton, explained that if a wife maliciously killed her husband she committed petty treason, but if a husband maliciously killed his wife 'this is but murder'. The reason for the difference was 'that the one is in subjection, and oweth obedience, and not the other'. The punishment for a petty traitor was burning and John Evelyn recorded seeing 'a miserable creature burning, who had murdered her husband' in Smithfield in 1652.

The execution of wives as petty traitors was rare, but the statutes of 1563 against witchcraft and of 1624 against mothers concealing the death of illegitimate babies led to an increase in prosecution of women for these crimes. This has been described as part of the criminalization of women, but female offenders were in the minority in the secular courts and for this reason their prosecution for criminal activity in the period has been described as 'atypical' (Kermode & Walker 1994). Women were far more likely to appear before the Church courts, where they could be charged with either religious or moral transgressions or where they were involved in the business of proving wills as executrices. Women were also more likely to bring cases, most commonly of defamation, in the Church courts, which were relatively cheap and fast. The pattern of prosecutions against women and the recourse which they had to the law as plaintiffs are important, not only to the investigation of court business, but also to our understanding of women's roles within society more generally. A number of modern studies have emphasized the active role taken by women in defining and defending the acceptable boundaries of neighbourly behaviour within their communities and their use of the law courts was an important part of this process.

In her work on the Cheshire criminal courts, Garthine Walker has argued that women's criminality should be considered within the context of their wider social and economic roles. Women were commonly prosecuted for stealing linen, clothes and household goods, which reflected their access to such items, their knowledge of their value and how to dispose of them. Women were also involved in detecting thefts in their neighbourhoods and in testifying against the accused. Laura Gowing has similarly argued that women's use of the Church courts to defend themselves against defamation or to prosecute their neighbours for immoral or disorderly behaviour should be interpreted as evidence of women's 'specific claims to authority in the household and the community' (Walker 1994; Gowing 1994, 1996). Although female participation in the courts was mediated through the agency of male justices and clerks, women should not be seen simply as passive and subordinate in the face of legal institutions that were run by men. Women were active as perpetrators of crime, as accusers and as witnesses.

One problem in assessing women's experience of the law courts is that their legal responsibilities were not the same as those of men. Some authorities believed that married women could not be held responsible for their actions. It has also been suggested that a woman who committed crimes with a male accomplice was less likely than the man to be prosecuted, especially if he were her husband. In his handbook for magistrates, *Eirenarcha, or of the office of the justices of peace* (1581), the Kent magistrate William Lambarde argued that if a woman was compelled by her husband to steal another man's goods she had not committed a felony, but if the husband had merely commanded her to steal then she had. It was an important distinction, because felony was punishable by death and before 1624 women were not allowed to plead benefit of clergy, a privilege which allowed men to escape the death sentence for a first offence of theft or manslaughter. The 1624 statute 'concerning Women convicted of small felonies' gave women the same right as men in cases of theft of money, goods or chattels valued at over one shilling and below ten shillings, or as an accessory to such an offence. Like men they were to be branded on the left hand with the letter T and could be imprisoned for up to a year. It was not legal to claim benefit more than once hence the need for branding. The statute was thought necessary because 'many women do suffer death for small causes' (SR: 21 Jac. I, cap. 6).

There were other ways in which women might escape the death penalty. The theft of goods valued at less than a shilling was petty larceny, for which the usual punishment was whipping. The courts frequently undervalued goods in order to allow minor thieves to escape the more severe punishment attached to grand larceny. Women faced with the death penalty also had the right to claim a stay of execution if they were pregnant, and Sharpe suggests that most women who 'pleaded the belly' were later fully pardoned (Sharpe 1984).

The inconsistency between the treatment of men and women was evident in the case of food riots and other assemblies. In *Eirenarcha* William Lambarde quoted Thomas Marrow's judgement of 1505 that the legislation against riot and unlawful assemblies was not applicable 'if a number of women or infants (under the age of discretion) do assemble themselves for their own cause', but if a man caused them 'to assemble to commit an unlawful act, then it is otherwise'. He recalled that a few years previously some women were 'worthily' punished in the Star Chamber, because 'having put off their seemly shamefastness, & apparelling themselves in the attire of men' a great number had then pulled down an enclosure.

There are numerous well documented cases of communal action by women to secure grain at fair prices or to prevent enclosure of previously common land. Contemporaries had a vested interest in claiming that men had directed or otherwise supported the women, because they could then be prosecuted, but there is no reason to doubt that women were capable of recognizing and defending communal rights. The most well analyzed example of food riots involving women took place in Maldon, Essex, in 1629 when over a hundred women boarded a Flemish ship and forced the crew to fill their caps and aprons with grain. The participants were treated leniently, but a few weeks later a crowd of two to three hundred men and women attacked the grain boats, and the ringleaders, including Ann Carter and four men, were sentenced to be hanged (Walter 1980).

The most widespread opposition to enclosures was provoked by the early seventeenth-century projects to drain the fenlands. In 1629 a crowd of some 350 mainly female commoners from Haxey, Lincolnshire, was involved in fierce opposition to drainage works undertaken by Sir Cornelius Vermuyden. Thirteen of the rioters, of whom nine were women, were later heavily fined in Star Chamber. Despite the serious punishments meted out in this and the Maldon case, it was popularly believed that women would be able to avoid the legal consequences of such actions. In 1567 up to thirty women were involved in destroying ditches and hedges at Wooburn, Buckinghamshire, when they discovered that their cattle had been beaten out of newly enclosed common land. It was said they had been advised by a man that 'women were lawless and might better do it' (Lindley 1982; Houlbrooke 1986).

Such beliefs may have been encouraged by the low rates of prosecution of women for other crimes. Carol Wiener's survey of Hertfordshire between 1589 and 1603 shows that women represented only 15 per cent of the indictments at quarter sessions and 14 per cent at the assizes for various sorts of theft. Women accounted for under 5 per cent of the prosecutions for commercial offences in these courts (Wiener 1975). It would be unwise, however, to conclude from these figures that women actually committed 15 per cent or less of all known incidents of these offences. Crime, local disputes and immorality alike were all under-reported whether through concealment, the leniency of the authorities towards women or out-of-court settlements.

Many minor offences or disputes never reached the courts because there was still great emphasis on conciliation between contending parties. The 1559 Elizabethan injunctions specifically defined one of the roles of the clergy as the reconciliation of neighbours. Women may have had a particularly prominent role to play as local peacemakers, but the whole process went largely unrecorded. In his *Breviate of the life of Margaret . . . wife of Richard Baxter* (1681) Baxter admitted that his wife was better at solving parishioners' problems than 'most divines that ever I knew in my life'. Abundant cases of conscience were brought to Baxter, 'some about restitution, some about injuries, some about references, some about vows, some about marriage promises, and many such like' and he referred all but the confidential cases to her for advice (Eales 1990b).

Not only the clergy, but also the laity were involved in the process of conciliation. After her death the Countess of Warwick was described by Anthony Walker in her funeral sermon *The virtuous woman found* (1683) as 'the arbitress and umpiress of all the controversies among her neighbours: many of which she happily and successfully reconciled and decided their quarrels both with wisdom and equity'. Walker pointed out that it was unusual for a woman to behave in such an authoritative way. Nevertheless, women of lower social status may have played their parts in defusing local problems before they got to court, just as they were to play an active role in bringing other crimes such as infanticide or witchcraft to light.

Infanticide was a crime which women were particularly believed to be likely to try to conceal. It was also associated with sexual immorality and the authorities were keen to punish women who tried to conceal the birth of an illegitimate child. Sharpe has pointed out that fewer Englishwomen may have been executed for witchcraft than for infanticide and notes that, between 1580 and 1709 in Cheshire, 33 women were hanged for infanticide compared with 11 men and women for witchcraft (Sharpe 1984). The majority of those accused of infanticide, some 90 per cent, were the mothers of the dead child. The murder of children was recognized as a felony, but the 1624 statute 'to prevent murdering of bastard children' focused on the covert disposal of illegitimate newborns by their mothers. The act alleged that 'many lewd' women had secretly murdered their bastard offspring under the pretence of stillbirth. According to the terms of the new legislation a woman who concealed the dead body of an illegitimate baby was guilty of murder unless a witness could prove that the child had died naturally (SR: 21 Jac. I, cap. 27).

After 1624 the force of the law was directed at detecting infanticide by unmarried mothers rather than by married women. Wrightson has argued that the practice was used to dispose of a minority of 'unwanted, predominantly illegitimate, children' either at birth or through subsequent neglect. His conclusion is based on the assize files for Essex, which record 60 cases between 1601 and 1665, in which all but one of the accused mothers were unmarried and 53 of the victims were clearly illegitimate. Just under half of the accused, 29, were found guilty and were sentenced to death. The crime was unlikely, Wrightson argues, to have been used as a method of population control, although he concedes that married women would have been able to hide the crime more easily (Hoffer & Hull 1981; Wrightson 1975). The fact that so few married women were prosecuted means that it is also difficult to assess whether unwanted female children were disposed of by infanticide. An unmarried woman motivated by shame or guilt would rid herself of the child no matter what its sex. This is borne out by the Essex sample cited above in which 29 of the victims were male and 33 were female, but married couples who wanted sons might well have disposed of or neglected daughters and these cases are not so easy to trace.

By the late seventeenth century, accused women were increasingly able to mount successful defences against the charge of infanticide. In 1673 Ann Jewring, a single mother who had concealed her pregnancy and the death of her infant, whose body was found hidden in a box, escaped charges on the grounds that she had prepared linen for the baby before its birth. After 1700 such a defence was almost guaranteed to succeed as long as there were no signs of violence on the baby's body. Conviction rates began to fall from the late seventeenth century and this was in keeping with eighteenth century jurors' increasing refusal to convict in all types of murder cases. Similarly jurors became more willing to believe that bruises and cuts on a child's body were caused by accident rather than design. The statute of 1624 was repealed in 1803, although concealment of the birth of a stillborn child could still be punished by two years' imprisonment (Hoffer & Hull 1981).

Just as the law against infanticide was less rigorously enforced from the late seventeenth century, so other laws were not always fully exercised. In 1604 bigamy was made a felony and prosecution moved from the Church courts to the crown courts, but the death penalty was rarely invoked. Twenty-one cases of bigamy have been traced in the court records in Essex in the seventeenth century and these involved accusations against seventeen men, one of whom was hanged, and four women, three of whom were sentenced to hang, but were reprieved. Adultery with a married woman and incest were similarly made felonies by the Parliamentary ordinance of 1650, which also made fornication punishable by three months' imprisonment, but again this legislation was not widely enforced. Only seven people were indicted in Essex for adultery in the 1650s and none suffered the death penalty, while only six people were imprisoned for fornication. There seems to have been no popular demand for such harsh measures against sexual offenders and the Adultery Act was repealed at the Restoration (Sharpe 1983; Thomas 1978; Durston 1989).

Similarly, before the statute of 1563 against witchcraft the Church courts had dealt with most cases of witchcraft and sorcery, such as the early Elizabethan examples of Agnes Frencham and Joan Gore of Sutton Valence, Kent, who used the 'sieve and shears' as a method of divining, and Joan Harper of Ash, Kent, who was forced publicly to abjure 'unlawful arts or devilish practices' (Willis 1975). Although it has been suggested that English witchcraft was regarded largely as malicious (*maleficium*) and that charges of Satanism were mainly a continental refinement, it is clear that fears of Devil-worship were present in witchcraft cases in the sixteenth century and these fears were reinforced by the early Stuart legislation. In England a statute against witchcraft was briefly in force between 1542 and 1547, but the most important acts were passed by Parliament in 1563 and 1604. From 1563 witchcraft was defined as a felony, if it resulted in the death of a person on the first offence or the harm of a person or their goods on a second offence. The 1604 measure was harsher and made harm a felony on the first offence and the invocation of spirits punishable by death.

Numerous causes have been put forward to explain the increase in trials for witchcraft, including Protestantism, the Counter-Reformation and the transition to capitalism (Trevor-Roper 1969; Thomas 1971). Explanations which focus specifically on why women were the majority of the accused have suggested it resulted from a fear of women who did not conform to the patriarchal ideal, the oppression of women and psychological fear of women's maternal power. One of the most convincing interpretations is contained in the work of Diane Purkiss, who draws on the insights of pyschoanalysis to explain the witch as a focus of women's own anxieties about their roles as mothers and providers (Larner 1981; Hester 1992; Willis 1995; Purkiss 1996). It was certainly believed that witches were more likely to be female than male and as many as 90 per cent of those accused in England were women. It has been estimated that between 500 and 1,000 people suffered the death penalty as witches in England between 1563 and 1736, while in Europe as a whole the figure was in the region of 50,000 to 60,000 (Geis and Bunn 1997; Sharpe 1996).

Reginald Scot suggested in *Discovery of witchcraft* (1584) that post-menopausal women were particularly at risk of being accused of the crime 'upon the stopping of their monthly melancholic flux or issue of blood' as this made them prone to the vain imagination that they could command the Devil. Although there is no evidence that there were organized networks of covens in early modern England, the testimony of the accused suggests that some people believed that they could harness supernatural powers. The existence of cunning men and women who used magic and herbal knowledge to cure illness or to retrieve lost or stolen items argues for the popular acceptance of such powers. Scot was, however, unusually sceptical and argued that if witches could control supernatural forces then why did they remain poor, old and friendless? His stereotype of the accused witch has been confirmed by scholarly research, which suggests that the accused were likely to be older women, living alone, who were of lower social status than those who accused them. Witchcraft was also a largely rural phenomenon that was contained within local communities and it was rare for an unknown outsider to be accused of the crime.

Thomas and Macfarlane have argued that witchcraft accusations arose because of the breakdown of traditional forms of neighbourliness and charity in the post-Reformation period. Not only were Catholic forms of face-to-face almsgiving removed, to be replaced by centralized poor law relief, but the constraints of inflation and economic reorganization in the sixteenth century led to a reluctance amongst communities to support the poverty-stricken old women in their midst. Both historians have rejected the interpretation of witch prosecutions as part of a sex war waged by men against women, since so many of the victims and accusers were female. This last point was initially answered by Larner, in relation to Scottish witch trials, who argued that women competed for male approval by accusing those who did not conform of being witches (Thomas 1971; Macfarlane 1970; Larner 1981).

Holmes has also noted that although women were witnesses and accusers, they played an ancillary role and the process of bringing a case to court was usually orchestrated by men. Sharpe has emphasized the extent to which prosecutions originated in disputes between women, specifically in arenas of female activity such as childcare or nursing the sick. He has suggested that in some instances trials were the result of inter-generational conflict between younger and older women. While acknowledging that accusations hinged upon the misogynistic interpretation of women as morally weaker than men and more likely to succumb to the temptation of evil, Sharpe also argues that the operation of these popular beliefs was complex and subtle. In particular he draws attention to the nature of the power of supposed witches, which centred on their ability to inflict damage, injury and death through the use of curses.

There is an instructive parallel here with defamation, which involved slander of an individual's reputation, usually by attacking their sexual probity. In both witchcraft and defamation cases, and even scolding, the use of a verbal assault was seen as serious, whether in terms of physical injury or of damage to a person's good name. Holmes has similarly emphasized the fear generated by accused witches within their communities that led to them being uneasily tolerated for a considerable time before court action was taken against them. This last point helps to account for the fact that young people were not generally accused, as it took some time before an individual gained a reputation as a witch and before a community was incited to act against their supposedly dangerous powers (Holmes 1993; Sharpe 1991, 1996).

The contribution of Purkiss to this debate highlights the depositions of women as sources of information about the meanings they attached to witchcraft. Although the testimony of witnesses was elicited and recorded by male court officials, their evidence shows rural women inhabiting a culture in which the exchange of food and utensils was crucial to their economic survival and where rituals of childbirth and churching marked a vulnerable point in the female life cycle. The events which triggered witchcraft accusations, such as the preparation of food or child care, are well known, but Purkiss emphasizes the psychological importance of these events for women. Loss of control over routine domestic tasks or the death of a child raised powerful female anxieties, which were expressed in fear of the evil witch as the opposite of the good wife or mother. Whereas most historians have been concerned with portraying the witch as the enemy of the Church or of men, Purkiss incisively demonstrates how the figure of the witch was defined by women at a popular level as a threat to them within their own homes. She thus demonstrates an important division between elite and popular perceptions of witchcraft (Purkiss 1996).

The decline of the witch trials from the late seventeenth century has been attributed to changing attitudes amongst the elite, who would no longer allow cases to be prosecuted through the courts. The last conviction of a witch at an English assize court was that of Jane Wenham in Hertfordshire in 1712 and, although she was found guilty by the jury, the judge obtained her reprieve. The English and Scottish witchcraft laws were repealed in 1736, but traditional popular beliefs about the power of witches have persisted in one form or another into the twentieth century (Sharpe 1996; Purkiss 1996).

The interpretations of Purkiss and Sharpe suggest that women were active agents in determining who should be classified as a witch in their local community, not only as accusers and witnesses, but also as searchers for the so-called witch's mark. The role of women as arbiters of acceptable social behaviour is also apparent in the use that some of them made of the courts to defend their reputations. Sometimes this was against the accusation of witchcraft, but more often it concerned slanders of a sexual nature. From the late sixteenth until the late seventeenth century cases of defamation came to dominate business in the Church courts between parties and the majority of cases were brought by women against other women. Gowing has found that, by 1633, 70 per cent of the London diocesan court cases between parties concerned defamation and, of those, 80 per cent were sued by women usually against other women. Similar trends have been detected by Ingram in Wiltshire and by Sharpe in the York diocesan courts.

Women who fought defamation suits were largely from the middling ranks in society and were usually married or widowed. Sharpe has emphasized that for female plaintiffs defamation usually consisted of descriptions of sexual immorality often containing the word 'whore'. He cites the case of Jane Marret, a York spinster, who was described by another woman as a 'hot arsed bitch, or hot arsed whore, or hot arsed quean, or some words to the very same effect' as typical. He also highlights the importance of their sexual honour to women and their male relatives, which led them to bring cases against their defamers. Sharpe also stresses that gossip played an important function as a form of social control or 'normative restriction'. Gowing sees gender as central to the issue of defamation as the words used to slander sexual honesty such as 'whore', 'jade', 'quean' or 'poxy whore' were all aimed at the behaviour of women whereas the words aimed at men were not about their promiscuity, but about their control over women's sexuality such as 'whoremaster', 'pander' or 'cuckold'. Gowing, like Sharpe, demonstrates that women were anxious to defend their sexual reputations, but also that they used gossip, defamatory words and the Church courts to curtail the immoral or otherwise unacceptable behaviour of their neighbours.

These cases of defamation illustrate an area where women were actively involved in prosecuting offenders. Women were less likely to prosecute their assailants in cases of rape, which was a felony and was regarded as so serious that offenders were not allowed benefit of clergy. The statute 18 Elizabeth I, cap. 7 defined rape as the 'unlawful and carnal knowledge' of any woman above the age of ten against her will, or of a female aged ten or under with or against her will. Rape was infrequently brought before the courts and in Essex Sharpe identified 36 men accused of rape between 1620 and 1680. Seven were found guilty (six of whom were hanged), fifteen were acquitted and eighteen were found *ignoramus*.

Given the severity of the punishment it is hard to agree with Gowing's broader conclusion that 'the stories that men told about sex automatically received more credit than those of women'. The legal authorities were aware of the need to balance the difficulties involved for a woman in proving that rape had taken place with those of an innocent man in defending himself. Women were urged to report rape as soon as possible and Dalton advised a woman who was raped 'presently to levy hue and cry or to complain thereof to some credible persons' and at the end of the eighteenth century Blackstone noted that juries would not 'give credit to a stale complaint'. Nevertheless, Sharpe suggests that all sexual offences were seriously under-reported (Sharpe 1983).

The situation was further complicated in the matter of rape because it was commonly believed that if the victim became pregnant, then in the words of Dalton 'this is no rape for a woman cannot conceive with child except she do consent'. This reflects the commonly held view that both men and women ejaculated 'seed' at orgasm without which conception could not occur. A woman must therefore have experienced sexual pleasure in order to conceive and she could not claim that she had been raped. Women undoubtedly failed to report rape through fear of their assailant or in the belief that their word would not be believed.

A parallel situation existed in the case of women who were beaten by their husbands. It was widely recognized that heads of households had the right to beat their subordinates and in law this included a man's wife, but the Church took an altogether different view. The *Homily on the state of matrimony* argued that there were no circumstances in which a husband should use blows against his wife and the majority of clerical authors followed this advice. Women were therefore likely to complain of violent husbands to the Church courts, whose penalties, although light, might shame the offender. A typical case was that of Thomas Frenchebourn of Westwell, Kent, who early in Elizabeth's reign was accused of tying his wife, Ann, to a post and beating her and thrusting a bodkin into her head. He was admonished by the Canterbury diocesan courts to end dissension with his wife and was fined two shillings.

Historians have frequently argued that a double standard operated in connection with sexual offences, whereby men's lapses were ignored or treated more leniently than those of women (Thomas 1959). The history of crime suggests that a reverse double standard operated in terms of the prosecution of women for criminal transgressions. The legal status of women was not the same as that of men and in the case of a married woman her husband might be forced to take responsibility for her religious or financial misdealings. Although the disadvantages of women before the law have received a great deal of attention, these have not always been weighed against the advantages that they could claim.

In particular the statutes of 1563 against witchcraft and of 1624 against concealing the deaths of illegitimate babies have been cited as evidence of the criminalization of women in the early modern period. Yet the statute of 1563 does not specifically link women with the crime of witchcraft and in 1624 benefit of clergy was also extended to women, a concession that has been little analyzed. Women were in general regarded as less likely to commit crime than men and apart from the more sensational felonies, their prosecution formed only a minority of cases in the secular courts. Their use of the Church courts to redress cases of defamation and even wife-beating demonstrates that they were able to mould ecclesiastical court practice to the defence of both their honour and in some cases their persons.

Conclusion

The preceding chapters have highlighted issues of debate amongst historians, as well as areas where more research is needed before overall conclusions about the lives of women in the early modern era can be drawn. In particular Underdown's postulation that the period witnessed a crisis in gender relations needs to be tested against considerably more regional enquiry. It can be stated, however, that the older historical narratives outlined in Chapter One have not been sustained by the research of the past three decades. The belief that women's spiritual status was elevated by the Reformation has been vigorously challenged by the counter-argument that patriarchal norms were reinforced by Protestant teaching. The thesis that the seventeenth century saw a decline in women's economic status has also been replaced by a more complex picture of variation between regions and within trades.

In any case, the search for one over-arching theory that will explain the experiences of all women is misguided, since differences of rank or class meant that the status of women was not uniform. As Mary Astell wrote in the Preface to the 1706 edition of *Reflections upon marriage*, published during the reign of Queen Anne, it was absurd to argue that every man by nature was superior to every woman, because then the greatest queen 'ought not to command, but to obey her footman'. She continued that it was no great discovery to argue that some men are superior to some women, but also pointed out that some women are superior to some men and that 'one woman is superior to all the men in these nations'.

As Astell realized, considerations of class make it imperative that the history of women is not analyzed in isolation, but in relation to the history of men. Most early modern theorists may have regarded women as the inferior sex, but their works must be placed in the context of a religious framework which saw the whole of humanity as sinful since the Fall. Men and women were tainted by original sin, but they could attain salvation. A positive construction of femininity, based particularly on religious ideals, was thus developed alongside a more negative view, and the same can be said of constructions of masculine behaviour. Furthermore, the majority of men did not have access to the political power or the privileged education of the elite. Men's foremost concern was the economic survival of themselves and their families, an interest that was shared equally by women, and there were acknowledged paths by which women could assume responsibility for this and other family matters.

Religious scruple and the protection of family interests were the two key motivations which were claimed by women as legitimate justifications for their intervention in both private and public matters. The importance of the family as both an economic and political unit also meant that the boundaries between private and public were not clear cut. Much of the most influential prescriptive writing of the period was, however, produced by clerics, who argued for the separation of the domestic functions of women and the public duties of men. The clergy drew such clear cut lines not only on the basis of their personal view of marriage but also because their own ministerial function could not be exercised by women. These rigid, gendered demarcations, which held good for the clergy, did not reflect actual social practices among other groups.

Exceptional piety could be used by women to influence family, local and even national affairs. Women maintained and extended channels of patronage on behalf of their families through marriage negotiations, social contacts, and the exchange of gifts and letters. They could also act to preserve their families in times of dearth or economic constraint by protesting at high prices or the enclosure of common land. The management of childbirth and the rituals that followed were female concerns, and the knowledge that midwives and other women gained in this arena could be transferred to the regulation of local sexual and criminal activity. Women were also active in defining the boundaries of acceptable neighbourly behaviour through the use of gossip, and in defending their own reputations in the courts when those bounds were broken.

It is the task of historians not only to interpret the past, but also to explain why change took place. The Reformation and the English

Civil Wars did have a specific impact on women. The religious disputes generated by the Reformation gave women a legitimate basis from which to oppose the authorities of the Church and state, and even their own husbands if they differed in religious belief. This challenge to patriarchal authority was reinforced by the opposition to Charles I and his execution in 1649, for if a tyrannical king could be deposed so too could a tyrannical husband. Women participated vigorously in the political and religious disputes of the 1640s and 1650s and this prompted them to formulate the basis for a feminist critique of the political system of patriarchy.

The deaths inflicted by the fighting in the civil wars throughout the British Isles also had a practical long-term impact on women who were left to run families and businesses on their own. The death toll amongst men may well, for example, have opened opportunities of work to women in the second half of the seventeenth century. By 1700, as a result of the civil wars and the Glorious Revolution of 1688, the analogy between royal and paternal authority was under attack, but patriarchy as an institution was able to adapt and survive. The scientific enquiries of the seventeenth century led to a more secular interpretation of political and fatherly power; but it was the growth of liberal democratic ideals, as well as changes in scientific, educational and medical theories, that would eventually lead to the recognition of the political and civic rights of all adult men and women. The achievement of universal suffrage and the expansion of educational provision in the twentieth century have provided the basis for equality between the sexes, but the extent to which that equality is constrained by biological and psychological difference remains a matter for continued research and debate.

Bibliography

Adair, R. *Courtship, illegitimacy and marriage in early modern England*. Manchester: Manchester University Press, 1996.

Alexander, S. Women, class and sexual differences: some reflections on the writing of a feminist history. *History Workshop* 17, 1984.

Amussen, S. Gender, family and the social order, 1560–1725. See Fletcher & Stevenson (eds), 1985.

—— *An ordered society: family and village in England, 1560–1725*. Oxford: Basil Blackwell, 1988.

Armstrong, C. The piety of Cicely, Duchess of York: a study in late medieval culture. In *England, France and Burgundy in the fifteenth century*, C. Armstrong (ed.), London: Hambledon Press, 1983.

Aston, M. Lollard Women Priests? *Journal of Ecclesiastical History* 31, 1980.

Aughterson, K. *Renaissance woman: a sourcebook, constructions of femininity in England*. London: Routledge, 1995.

Axtell, J. *The educational writings of John Locke: a critical edition with introduction and notes*. Cambridge: Cambridge University Press, 1968.

Bainton, R. *Women of the Reformation in France and England*. Boston: Beacon Press, 1975.

Barron, C. The 'Golden Age' of women in medieval London. In *Medieval Women in southern England*. Reading, Berks: Reading Medieval Studies 15, 1989.

Beier, L. M. *Sufferers and healers: the experience of illness in seventeenth-century England*. London: Routledge, 1987.

Beilin, E. Anne Askew's self-portrait in the *Examinations*. See Hannay (ed.), 1985.

—— *Redeeming Eve: women writers of the English Renaissance*. Princeton, NJ: Princeton University Press, 1987.

113

Ben-Amos, I. *Adolescence and youth in early modern England*. New Haven, Conn: Yale University Press, 1994.

Bennett, H. *The Pastons and their England*. Cambridge: Cambridge University Press, 1968.

Bennett, J. History that stands still: women's work in the European past. *Feminist Studies* 14, 1988.

Bowden, C. Women as intermediaries: an example of the use of literacy in the late sixteenth and early seventeenth centuries. *History of Education* 22, 1993.

Bray, A. *Homosexuality in Renaissance England*. New York: Columbia University Press, 1995.

Bruyn, L. de *Woman and the devil in sixteenth-century literature*. Tisbury, Wilts: The Compton Press, 1979.

Cahn, S. *Industry of devotion: the transformation of women's work in England, 1500–1660*. New York: Columbia University Press, 1987.

Carlton, C. *Going to the wars: the experience of the British Civil Wars, 1638–1651*. London: Routledge, 1992.

Cerasano, S. P. & Wynne-Davies, M. *Renaissance drama by women: texts and documents*. London: Routledge, 1996.

Charles, C. & Duffin, L. (eds). *Women and work in pre-industrial England*. Beckenham, Kent: Croom Helm, 1985.

Clark, A. *Working life of women in the seventeenth century*. London: Routledge, 1992.

Clark, P. The ownership of books in England, 1560–1640: the example of some Kentish townsfolk. In *Schooling and Society: Studies in the History of Education*, L. Stone (ed.). Baltimore: Johns Hopkins University Press, 1976.

Clarke, S. *A looking-glass for good women to dress themselves by: held forth in the life and death of Mrs Katherine Clarke*. London, 1677.

Claydon, T. *William III and the Godly Revolution*. Cambridge: Cambridge University Press, 1996.

Clinton, E. *The Countess of Lincoln's nursery*. London, 1622.

Coleman, D. *The economy of England, 1450–1750*. Oxford: Oxford University Press, 1977.

Collinson, P. The role of women in the English Reformation illustrated by the life and friendships of Anne Locke. In *Godly people: essays on English Protestantism and puritanism*, P. Collinson (ed.). London: Hambledon Press, 1983.

—— *The birthpangs of Protestant England: religious and cultural change in the sixteenth and seventeenth centuries.* London: Macmillan Press, 1988.

Corfield, P. History and the challenge of gender history. *Rethinking History* 1, 1997.

Crawford, P. Women's published writings, 1600–1700. See Prior (ed.), 1985.

—— *Women and religion in England, 1500–1720.* London: Routledge, 1993.

Cresswell, A. *The Dering love letters.* Maidstone, Kent: Kent County Council, 1994.

Cressy, D. *Education in Tudor and Stuart England.* London: Edward Arnold, 1975.

—— *Literacy and the social order.* Cambridge: Cambridge University Press, 1980.

—— Kinship and kin interaction in early modern England. *Past and Present* 113, 1986.

—— *Coming over: Migration and communication between England and New England in the seventeenth century.* Cambridge: Cambridge University Press, 1987.

—— *Birth, marriage and death: ritual, religion, and the life-cycle in Tudor and Stuart England.* Oxford: Oxford University Press, 1997.

Cross, C. 'Great reasoners in scripture': the activities of women Lollards, 1380–1530. In *Medieval women*, D. Baker (ed.). Oxford: Basil Blackwell, 1978.

—— The religious life of women in sixteenth-century Yorkshire. See Sheils & Wood (eds), 1990.

Davies, K. M. The sacred condition of equality – how original were puritan doctrines of marriage? *Social History*, 5, 1977.

—— Continuity and change in literary advice on marriage. See Outhwaite (ed.), 1981.

Davis, N. Z. 'Women's history' in transition: the European case. *Feminist Studies* 3, 1976.

Dolan, F. *Dangerous familiars: representations of domestic crime in England, 1550–1700.* Ithaca, New York: Cornell University Press, 1994.

Doran, S. *Monarchy and matrimony: the courtships of Elizabeth I.* London: Routledge, 1996.

Dowling, M. A woman's place? Learning and the wives of Henry VIII. *History Today* 41, 1991.

Duffy, E. Holy maydens, holy wyfes: the cult of women saints in fifteenth- and sixteenth-century England. See Sheils and Wood (eds), 1990.

Durston, C. *The family in the English Revolution*. Oxford: Basil Blackwell, 1989.

Dyer, A. *Decline and growth in English towns, 1400–1640*. London: Macmillan Press, 1991.

Eales, J. *Puritans and roundheads: the Harleys of Brampton Bryan and the outbreak of the English Civil War*. Cambridge: Cambridge University Press, 1990a.

—— Samuel Clarke and the 'lives' of godly women in seventeenth-century England. See Sheils and Wood (eds), 1990b.

—— The family and kinship. *Early Modern History* 1, 1992.

—— Gender construction in early modern England and the conduct books of William Whately (1583–1639). In *Gender and Christian Religion*: R. Swanson (ed.). *Studies in Church History*, 34. Woodbridge, Suffolk: Boydell and Brewer, 1998.

Earle, P. *The making of the English middle class: business, society and family life in London, 1660–1730*. London: Methuen, 1989.

Eccles, A. *Obstetrics and gynaecology in Tudor and Stuart England*. London: Croom Helm, 1982.

Erickson, A. *Women and property in early modern England*. London: Routledge, 1993.

The Europa biographical dictionary of British women, A. Crawford, T. Hayter, A. Hughes, F. Prochaska, P. Stafford and E. Vallance (eds). London: Europa, 1983.

Evenden, D. Mothers and their midwives in seventeenth-century London. In *The art of midwifery: early modern midwives in Europe*, H. Marland (ed.). London: Routledge, 1993.

Ezell, M. *The patriarch's wife: literary evidence and the history of the family*. Chapel Hill, NC: University of North Carolina Press, 1987.

Ferguson, M. *First feminists: British women writers, 1578–1799*. Bloomington, Ind: Indiana University Press, 1985.

Fildes, V. *Wet nursing: a history from antiquity to the present*. Oxford: Basil Blackwell, 1988.

—— (ed.). *Women as mothers in pre-industrial England*. London: Routledge, 1990.

Fletcher, A. The Protestant idea of marriage. In *Religion, culture and society in early modern Britain*, Fletcher, A. & Roberts, P. (eds). Cambridge: Cambridge University Press, 1994.

—— Men's dilemma: the future of patriarchy in England, 1560–1660. *Transactions of the Royal Historical Society*, Sixth Series, 4: 61–81, 1995a.

—— *Gender, sex and subordination in England, 1500–1800*. New Haven, Conn. & London: Yale University Press, 1995b.

—— & Stevenson, J. (eds). *Order and disorder in early modern England*. Cambridge: Cambridge University Press, 1985.

Fraser, A. *The weaker vessel: woman's lot in seventeenth-century England*. London: Weidenfeld & Nicolson, 1984.

Friedman, A. The influence of humanism on the education of girls and boys in Tudor England. *History of Education Quarterly* 39, 1985.

Gardiner, D. *English girlhood at school: a study of women's education through twelve centuries*, Oxford: Oxford University Press, 1929.

Geis, G. and Bunn, I. *A trial of witches: a seventeenth-century witchcraft prosecution*. London: Routledge, 1997.

Gentles, I. *The New Model Army in England, Ireland and Scotland, 1645–1653*. Oxford: Basil Blackwell, 1992.

George, M. *Women in the first capitalist society: experiences in seventeenth-century England*. Urbana, Ill: University of Illinois Press, 1988.

Gibson, G. M. Saint Anne and the religion of childbed: some East Anglian texts and talismans. In *Interpreting cultural symbols: Saint Anne in late medieval society*. Ashley, K. and Sheingorn, P. (eds). Athens, Georgia: University of Georgia Press, 1990.

Gilchrist, R. *Gender and material culture: the archaeology of religious women*. London: Routledge, 1994.

Goldberg, P. *Women, work and life cycle in a medieval economy: women in York and Yorkshire, c. 1300–1520*. Oxford: Clarendon Press, 1992.

Gowing, L. Language, power, and the law: women's slander litigation in early modern London. See Kermode & Walker (eds), 1994.

—— *Domestic dangers: women, words, and sex in early modern London*. Oxford: Oxford University Press, 1996.

Haigh, C. *Elizabeth I*. London: Longman, 1988.

—— *English reformations: religion, politics and society under the Tudors*. Oxford: Oxford University Press, 1993.

Hair, P. E. H. Bridal pregnancy in rural England in earlier centuries. *Population Studies* 20, 1966–7.

—— Bridal pregnancy in earlier rural England further examined. *Population Studies* 24, 1970.

Hallam, E. Turning the hourglass: gender relations at the deathbed in early modern Canterbury. *Mortality* 1, 1996.

Haller, W. & Haller, M. The puritan art of love. *Huntington Library Quarterly* 5, 1942.

Hannay, M. (ed.). *Silent but for the Word: Tudor women as patrons, translators, and writers of religious works*. Kent, Ohio: Kent State University Press, 1985.

—— 'How I these studies prize': The Countess of Pembroke and Elizabethan science. See Hunter & Hutton (eds), 1997.

Harley, D. Historians as demonologists: the myth of the midwife–witch. *Social History of Medicine* 3, 1990.

Harris, B. Women and politics in early Tudor England. *The Historical Journal* 33, 1990.

Harris. F. The electioneering of Sarah, Duchess of Marlborough. *Parliamentary History* 2, 1983.

—— *A passion for government: the life of Sarah, Duchess of Marlborough*. Oxford: Oxford University Press, 1991.

Henderson, K. & McManus, B. *Half-humankind: contexts and texts of the controversy about women in England, 1540–1640*. Urbana and Chicago, Ill.: University of Illinois Press, 1985.

Hester, M. *Lewd women and wicked witches: a study of the dynamics of male domination*. London: Routledge, 1992.

Higgins, P. The reactions of women, with special reference to women petitioners. In *Politics, religion and the English Civil War*, B. Manning (ed.). London: Edward Arnold, 1973.

Hill, B. *The first English feminist: 'Reflections upon marriage' and other writings by Mary Astell*. Aldershot, Hants: Gower, 1986.

—— *Women, work and sexual politics in eighteenth-century England*. Oxford: Basil Blackwell, 1989.

Hill, C. *Society and puritanism in pre-revolutionary England*. London: Secker & Warburg, 1964.

Hinds, H. *God's Englishwomen: seventeenth-century radical sectarian writing and feminist criticism*. Manchester: Manchester University Press, 1996.

Hobby, E. *Virtue of necessity: English women's writing, 1649–1688*. London: Virago, 1988.

Hoffer, P. & Hull, N. *Murdering mothers: infanticide in England and New England, 1558–1803*. New York: New York University Press, 1981.

Holderness, B. *Pre-industrial England: economy and society from 1500 to 1750*. London: Dent, 1976.

Holmes, C. Women: witnesses and witches. *Past and Present* **140**, 1993.

Houlbrooke, R. *Church courts and the people during the English Reformation, 1520–1570*. Oxford: Oxford University Press, 1979.

—— *The English family, 1450–1700*. London: Longman, 1984.

—— Women's social life and common action in England from the fifteenth century to the eve of the Civil War. *Continuity and Change* **1**, 1986.

Hughes, A. Gender and politics in Leveller literature. In *Political culture and cultural politics in early modern Europe*, S. Amussen and M. Kishlansky (eds). Manchester: Manchester University Press, 1995.

Hughes, P. & Larkin, J. *Tudor royal proclamations: the early Tudors, 1485–1553*. New Haven, Conn: Yale University Press, 1964.

Hull, S. *Chaste, silent and obedient: English books for women, 1475–1640*. San Marino, Cal: Huntington Library, 1982.

Hunter, L. & Hutton, S. *Women, science and medicine, 1500–1700*. Stroud, Glos: Alan Sutton, 1997.

Hussey, A. *Testamenta Cantiana: a series of extracts from fifteenth- and sixteenth-century wills relating to church building and topography: East Kent*. London: Mitchell Hughes & Clarke, 1907.

Hutton, S. Anne Conway, Margaret Cavendish and seventeenth-century scientific thought. See Hunter & Hutton (eds), 1997.

Ingram, M. Spousals litigation in the English ecclesiastical courts, *c.* 1350–1640. See Outhwaite (ed.), 1981.

—— *Church courts, sex and marriage in England, 1570–1640*. Cambridge: Cambridge University Press, 1987.

—— 'Scolding women cucked or washed': a crisis in gender relations in early modern England? See Kermode & Walker (eds), 1994.

Jackson, C. (ed.). *The autobiography of Mrs Alice Thornton of East Newton, co. York*. Durham: Surtees Society, **62**, 1873.

Jardine, L. *Still harping on daughters: women and drama in the age of Shakespeare*. Totowa, NJ: Barnes and Noble, 1983.

Joceline, E. *The mother's legacy to her unborn child*. London, 1624.

Jones, M. & Underwood, M. *The king's mother: Lady Margaret Beaufort, Countess of Richmond and Derby*. Cambridge: Cambridge University Press, 1992.

Keeble, N. H. (ed.). *The cultural identity of seventeenth-century woman: a reader*. London: Routledge, 1994.

Kelly, J. Did women have a Renaissance. In *Becoming visible: women in European history*, Bridenthal, R. & Koonz, C. (eds). Boston: Houghton Mifflin, 1977.

—— Early feminist theory and the *querelle des femmes*, 1400–1789. *Signs* 8, 1982.

Kelso, R. *Doctrine for the lady of the Renaissance*. Urbana, Ill. and Chicago: University of Illinois Press, 1956.

Kent, J. Attitudes of members of the House of Commons to the regulation of personal conduct in late Elizabethan and early Stuart England. *Bulletin of the Institute of Historical Research* 45, 1972.

Kermode, J. & Walker, G. (eds). *Women, crime and the courts in early modern England*. London: UCL Press, 1994.

Knowles, D. & Hadcock, N. *Medieval religious houses: England and Wales*. London: Longman, 1971.

Krontiris, T. *Oppositional voices: women as writers and translators of literature in the English Renaissance*. London: Routledge, 1992.

Kussmaul, A. *Servants in husbandry in early modern England*. Cambridge: Cambridge University Press, 1981.

Lacey, K. Women and work in fourteenth- and fifteenth-century London. See Charles and Duffin (eds), 1985.

Lake, P. Feminine piety and personal potency: the emancipation of Mrs Jane Ratcliffe. *Seventeenth Century* 2, 1987.

Lansberry, H. C. F. Free bench see-saw: Sevenoaks widows in the late seventeenth century. *Archaeologia Cantiana* 100, 1984.

Larner, C. *Enemies of God: the witch-hunt in Scotland*. London: Chatto & Windus, 1981.

Laslett, P. *Family life and illicit love in earlier generations*. Cambridge: Cambridge University Press, 1977.

—— *The world we have lost further explored*. London: Methuen, 1983.

Laurence, A. A priesthood of she-believers: women and congregations in mid-seventeenth century England. See Sheils & Wood (eds), 1990.

—— *Women in England, 1500–1760: a social history*. London: Weidenfeld and Nicolson, 1994.

Lerner, G. *The creation of patriarchy*. Oxford: Oxford University Press, 1986.

Levin, C. Women in *The Book of Martyrs* as models of behaviour in Tudor England. *International Journal of Women's Studies* 4, 1981.

—— *The heart and stomach of a king: Elizabeth I and the politics of sex and power*. Philadelphia: University of Pennsylvania Press, 1994.

Lewalski, B. K. Lucy, Countess of Bedford: images of a Jacobean courtier and patroness. In *Politics of discourse: the literature of seventeenth-century England*, K. Sharpe & S. Zwicker (eds). Berkeley, Cal: University of California Press, 1987.

Lewis, T. T. (ed.). *Letters of the Lady Brilliana Harley.* London: Camden Society, 1854.

Lindley, D. *The trials of Frances Howard.* London: Routledge, 1993.

Lindley, K. *Fenland riots and the English Revolution.* London: Heinemann, 1982.

Loftis, J. (ed.). *The memoirs of Anne, Lady Halkett and Ann, Lady Fanshawe.* Oxford: Oxford University Press, 1979.

Macek, E. The emergence of a feminine spirituality in *The Book of Martyrs. Sixteenth-Century Journal* 19, 1988.

Macfarlane, A. *Witchcraft in Tudor and Stuart England: a regional and comparative study.* London: Routledge & Kegan Paul, 1970.

—— *The origins of English individualism: the family, property and social transition.* Oxford: Basil Blackwell, 1978.

Mack, P. *Visionary women: ecstatic prophecy in seventeenth-century England.* Berkeley, Cal: University of California Press, 1992.

Maclean, I. *The Renaissance notion of woman: a study in the fortunes of scholasticism and medical science in European intellectual life.* Cambridge: Cambridge University Press, 1980.

Marsh, C. [and students]. *Songs of the seventeenth century.* Belfast: Queen's University of Belfast, 1995.

Mayor, J. (ed.). *The English works of John Fisher, Bishop of Rochester.* London: Early English Text Society, 1876.

McLaren, D. Marital fertility and lactation, 1570–1720. See Prior (ed.), 1985.

McLuskie, K. *Renaissance dramatists.* Hemel Hempstead, Herts: Harvester-Wheatsheaf, 1989.

McMullen, N. The education of English gentlewomen, 1540–1640. *History of Education* 6, 1977.

McSheffrey, S. *Gender and heresy: women and men in Lollard communities, 1420–1530.* Philadelphia: University of Pennsylvania Press, 1995.

Meads, D. *Diary of Lady Margaret Hoby, 1599–1605.* London: Routledge, 1930.

Meale, C. '. . . alle the bokes that I haue of latyn, englisch and frensch': laywomen and their books in late medieval England. In *Women and literature in Britain, 1150–1500*, C. Meale (ed.). Cambridge: Cambridge University Press, 1993.

Mendelson, S. Stuart women's diaries and occasional memoirs. See Prior (ed.), 1985.

Middleton, C. Women's labour and the transition to pre-industrial capitalism. See Charles and Duffin (eds), 1985.

Murphy, J. The illusion of decline: the privy chamber, 1547–1558. See Starkey (ed.), 1987.

Neale, J. *The Elizabethan House of Commons*. London: Jonathan Cape, 1949.

Neame, A. *The holy maid of Kent: The life of Elizabeth Barton, 1506–1534*. London: Hodder & Stoughton, 1971.

O'Day, R. *Education and society, 1500–1800*. London: Longman, 1982.

O'Hara, D. 'Ruled by my friends': aspects of marriage in the diocese of Canterbury, *c.* 1540–1570. *Continuity and Change* 6, 1991.

Oldham, J. On pleading the belly: a history of the jury of matrons. *Criminal Justice Yearbook* 6, 1985.

Outhwaite, R. B. (ed.). *Marriage and society: studies in the social history of marriage*. London: Europa, 1981.

—— *Clandestine marriage in England, 1500–1800*. London: Hambledon Press, 1995.

Pearson, J. Women reading, reading women. See Wilcox (ed.), 1996.

Perry, R. *The celebrated Mary Astell: an early English feminist*. Chicago: University of Chicago Press, 1986.

Phillips, R. *Untying the knot: a short history of divorce*. Cambridge: Cambridge University Press, 1991.

Pollock, L. 'Teach her to live under obedience': the making of women in the upper ranks of early modern England. *Continuity and Change* 4, 1989.

—— Embarking on a rough passage: the experience of pregnancy in early-modern society. See Fildes (ed.), 1990.

—— *With faith and physic: the life of a Tudor gentlewoman, Lady Grace Mildmay, 1552–1620*. London: Collins & Brown, 1993.

Power, E. *Medieval English nunneries c. 1275 to 1535*. Cambridge: Cambridge University Press, 1922.

—— *Medieval women*. Cambridge: Cambridge University Press, 1975.

Prior, M. (ed.) *Women in English society, 1500–1800*. London: Methuen, 1985.

Purkiss, D. *The witch in history*. London: Routledge, 1996.

Quaife, G. *Wanton wenches and wayward wives*. London: Croom Helm, 1979.

Rex, R. The execution of the holy maid of Kent. *Historical Research* **64**, 1991.

Riley, D. *'Am I that name?': feminism and the category of 'women' in history*. Basingstoke: Macmillan, 1988.

Rollins, H. (ed.). *A Pepysian garland: black-letter broadside ballads of the years 1595–1639 chiefly from the collection of Samuel Pepys*. Cambridge: Cambridge University Press, 1922.

Roper, L. *The holy household: women and morals in Reformation Augsburg*. Oxford: Oxford University Press, 1989.

Rowbotham, S. *Hidden from history: 300 years of women's oppression and the fight against it*. London: Pluto Press, 1973.

Rowlands, M. Recusant women, 1560–1640. See Prior (ed.), 1985.

Schochet, G. *Patriarchalism and political thought*. Oxford: Basil Blackwell, 1975.

Schücking, L. L. *The puritan family*. London: Routledge, 1969.

Schwoerer, L. Seventeenth-century English women engraved in stone? *Albion* **16**, 1984.

——— *Lady Rachel Russell: 'one of the best of women'*. Baltimore: John Hopkins, 1988.

Scott, J. Gender: a useful category of historical analysis. *American Historical Review* **91**, 1986.

Scott, J. W. *Gender and the politics of history*. New York: Columbia University Press, 1988.

Sharpe, J. *Defamation and sexual slander in early modern England: the Church courts at York*. York: Borthwick Papers **58**, 1980.

——— *Crime in seventeenth-century England: a county study*. Cambridge: Cambridge University Press, 1983.

——— *Crime in early modern England, 1550–1750*. London: Longman, 1984.

——— Witchcraft and women in seventeenth-century England: some northern evidence. *Continuity and Change* **6**, 1991.

——— *Instruments of darkness: witchcraft in England, 1550–1750*. London: Hamish Hamilton, 1996.

Sheils, W. & Wood, D. (eds). *Women in the Church: Studies in Church History* **27**. Oxford: Basil Blackwell, 1990.

Shephard, A. *Gender and authority in sixteenth-century England*. Keele, Staffs: Ryburn Publishing, 1994.

Shepherd, S. (ed.). *The women's sharp revenge.* London: Fourth Estate, 1985.

Slater, M. *Family life in the seventeenth century: the Verneys of Claydon House.* London: Routledge, 1984.

Smith, H. *Reason's disciples: seventeenth-century English feminists.* Urbana, Ill: University of Illinois Press, 1982.

Snell, K. *Annals of the labouring poor: social change and agrarian England, 1660–1900.* Cambridge: Cambridge University Press, 1985.

Sommerville, M. *Sex and subjection: attitudes towards women in early-modern Society.* London: Edward Arnold, 1995.

Souden, D. Migrants and the population structure of later seventeenth-century provincial cities and market towns. In *The transformation of English provincial towns*, P. Clark (ed.). London: Hutchinson, 1984.

Springborg, P. *Astell: political writings.* Cambridge: Cambridge University Press, 1996.

Spufford, M. First steps in literacy: the reading and writing experiences of the humblest seventeenth-century spiritual biographers. *Social History* 4, 1979.

—— *Small books and pleasant histories: popular fiction and its readership in seventeenth-century England.* Cambridge: Cambridge University Press, 1981.

St Clare Byrne, M. (ed.). *The Lisle letters* [6 vols]. Chicago: University of Chicago Press, 1981.

Starkey, D. (ed.). *The English court from the Wars of the Roses to the Civil War.* London: Longman, 1987.

Stephens, J. E. (ed.). *Aubrey on education.* London: Routledge, 1972.

Stone, L. The educational revolution in England, 1560–1640. *Past and Present* 28, 1964.

—— *The family, sex and marriage in England, 1500–1800.* London: Weidenfeld & Nicolson, 1977.

Stretton, T. Women, custom and equity in the Court of Requests. See Kermode & Walker (eds), 1994.

Sutherland, J. (ed.). *Lucy Hutchinson: memoirs of the life of Colonel Hutchinson with the fragment of an autobiography of Mrs Hutchinson.* Oxford: Oxford University Press, 1973.

Thomas, K. V. Women and the Civil War sects. *Past and Present* 13, 1958.

—— The double standard. *Journal of the History of Ideas* 20, 1959.

—— *Religion and the decline of magic: studies in popular belief in sixteenth- and seventeenth-century England*. London: Weidenfeld and Nicolson, 1971.

—— The puritans and adultery: The Act of 1650 reconsidered. In *Puritans and Revolutionaries*, D. Pennington & K. Thomas (eds). Oxford: Oxford University Press, 1978.

Todd, M. Humanists, puritans and the spiritualized household. *Church History* 49, 1980.

Trevett, C. *Women and Quakerism in the 17th century*. York: Ebor Press, 1991.

Trevor-Roper, H. *The European witch-craze of the sixteenth and seventeenth centuries*. London: Pelican Books, 1969.

Underdown, D. The taming of the scold: the enforcement of patriarchal authority in early modern England. See Fletcher & Stevenson (eds), 1985.

Vickery, A. Golden Age to separate spheres? A review of the categories and chronology of English women's history. *The Historical Journal* 36, 1993.

Walker, G. Women, theft and the world of stolen goods. See Kermode & Walker (eds), 1994.

Wall, A. Elizabethan precept and feminine practice: the Thynne family of Longleat. *History* 75, 1990.

Walter. J. Grain riots and popular attitudes to the law: Maldon and the crisis of 1629. In *An ungovernable people: the English and their law in the seventeenth and eighteenth centuries*, J. Brewer and J. Styles (eds). London: Hutchinson, 1980.

Ward, J. C. *English noblewomen in the later middle ages*. London: Longman, 1992.

Warren, A. K. *Anchorites and their patrons in medieval England*. Berkeley, Cal: University of California Press, 1985.

Watson, F. (ed.). *Vives and the Renascence education of women*. London: Edward Arnold, 1912.

Wiener, C. Sex roles and crime in late Elizabethan Hertfordshire. *Journal of Social History* 8, 1975.

Wiesner, M. *Gender, church and state in early modern Germany*. Harlow, Essex: Longman, 1998.

Wilcox, H. (ed.). *Women and literature in Britain, 1500–1700*. Cambridge: Cambridge University Press, 1996.

Willen, D. Women in the public sphere in early modern England: the case of the urban working poor. *Sixteenth-Century Journal* 19, 1988.

—— Women and religion in early modern England. In *Women in*

Reformation and Counter-Reformation Europe, S. Marshall (ed.). Bloomington, Ind: Indiana University Press, 1989.

Willis, A. J. *Church life in Kent being the Church court records of the Canterbury diocese, 1559–1565.* Chichester, Sussex: Phillimore, 1975.

Willis, D. *Malevolent nurture: witch-hunting and maternal power in early modern England.* Ithaca, New York: Cornell University Press, 1995.

Wilson, A. *The making of man-midwifery: childbirth in England, 1660–1770.* London: UCL Press, 1995.

Windeatt, B. A. *The book of Margery Kempe.* London: Penguin, 1985.

Wood, M. A. E. (ed.). *Letters of royal and illustrious ladies of Great Britain, from the commencement of the twelfth century to the close of the reign of Queen Mary* [3 vols]. London: Henry Colburn, 1846.

Woodbridge, L. *Women and the English Renaissance: literature and the nature of womankind, 1540–1620.* Urbana, Ill: University of Illinois Press, 1984.

Woodward, G. *Dissolution of the Monasteries.* London: Blandford Press, 1966.

Wright, P. A change in directions: the ramifications of a female household, 1558–1603. See Starkey (ed.), 1987.

Wright, S. 'Churmaids, huswyfes and hucksters': the employment of women in Tudor and Stuart Salisbury. Charles & Duffin (eds), 1985.

Wrightson, K. Infanticide in earlier seventeenth-century England. *Local Population Studies* 15, 1975.

—— *English society, 1580–1680.* London: Hutchinson, 1982.

—— & Levine, D. *Poverty and piety in an English village: Terling, 1525–1700.* London: Academic Press, 1979.

Wrigley, E. A. Urban growth and agricultural change. In R. I. Rotberg & T. K. Rabb (eds). *Population and economy*, Cambridge: Cambridge University Press, 1986.

– —— & Schofield, R. S. *The population history of England, 1541–1871: a reconstruction.* Cambridge: Cambridge University Press, 1989.

Youings, J. *The Dissolution of the Monasteries.* London: George Allen & Unwin, 1971.

Index

abortion 70
Abraham 24
Adam *see* Eve
adultery 12, 21, 27, 103
agriculture 75, 77
  pastoral regions 78
Agrippa, Heinrich 31, 42
alehouses 76, 81
Allen, William 48
Allestree, Richard 26
anatomy 3
anchoresses 90
Anger, Jane 16, 17
Anne of Denmark 39, 54
Anne, Queen (1702–14) 2, 58, 110
Anne, Saint 12, 88, 93
apprentices 39, 74, 79, 80
Aquinas, Thomas 23
Aragon, Katherine of *see* Katherine
  of Aragon
Aristotle 3, 23
Askew, Anne 16, 92, 95
Asteley, Catherine 53
Astell, Mary 18, 24, 33–4, 45, 110
Athaliah, Queen 49
d'Aubigny, Lady 55
Augustine, St 23, 36, 40
Aylmer, John 49–50

Bacon, Lady Ann *see* Cooke, Ann
Bale, John 92

ballads 24, 31–2, 34, 37, 60, 98
Ballard, George 9
baptism 87
Bardale, Clement 45
Barton, Elizabeth 90–1
Baxter, Margaret 67–8, 95, 101
Baxter, Richard 25, 26, 67–8, 101
Beaufort, Lady Margaret 16, 41, 51
Becon, Thomas 25, 26
Bedford, Lucy Countess of 54
Behn, Aphra 18, 42, 43,
benefit of clergy 99–100, 107, 109
Bertie, Richard 50, 52
bible 3, 5, 8, 31, 36, 40, 41, 42, 44,
  92
bigamy 102
Boccaccio, Giovanni 7
Boleyn, Anne 42, 51, 65
Boleyn, Mary 65–6
book of common prayer
  (1552) 70
  (1559) 24
books 23, 79, 97
  by women 16–18, 29, 32–4,
    43–5
  for women 28, 35, 36, 37–8
  ownership of by women 36,
    40–2
  see also bible, print culture
Bosworth, battle of (1485) 51
Bowyer, Elizabeth 70

Bradbelte, Dorothy 53, 54
breach of promise 21
breastfeeding 43, 69
  see also lactation, wet-nursing
Brettergh, Katherine 95
Bristol 80–1, 92
Bruen, John 95
Bulmer, Lady Margaret 51–2

Calvin, Jean 10, 42
Camden, William 8
Canterbury 68, 91
capitalism 6, 9, 73, 104
Carey, William 65
Carleton, Sir Dudley 54
Carlisle, Lucy Countess of see Hay, Lucy
Carr, Robert 53
Carter, Ann 100
Cary, Elizabeth, Viscountess Falkland 33, 35
catholic plot 55
catholic recusancy 21, 57, 86, 93–4
Catholicism 10, 11, 26, 32, 48–9, 50, 87–8, 91, 95–6, 105
Cavendish, Margaret, Duchess of Newcastle 18, 24, 33, 34, 43, 44
Cawdrey, Robert 38
Cecil, Robert 52
Cecil, William (Lord Burghley) 52, 54, 64
celibacy 10, 26
Cellier, Elizabeth 83
Chamberlain, Peter 82–3
Chambers, David 50
chapbooks 31–2
charivari (skimmington) 13, 78
Charles I (1625–49) 18, 44, 55, 96, 112
Chaucer, Geoffrey 7, 42
Cheshire 95, 102
Chidley, Katherine 56
childbirth 43, 70–1, 72, 88, 93, 106, 111

  see also midwives
christmas 32
Chudleigh, Lady Mary 45
Churchill, Sarah, Duchess of Marlborough 58–9
churching 70–1, 88, 106
churchwardens 88
Cicero 36
Clarendon, Earl of 56
Clark, Alice 9–10, 73, 84
Clark, Denis[e] 70
Clarke, Katherine (Overton) 9, 28, 71
Clarke, Samuel 9–10, 28,
Cleaver, Robert 25
clergy 10, 11–2, 25–29, 34, 35, 86, 95, 108
  as conciliators 101
  and private/public sphere 5, 28–9, 86, 111
  see also wives of clergy
Clifford, Lady Ann 39, 42
Clinton, Elizabeth, Countess of Lincoln 43, 62
Clitherow, Margaret 94
cloth trade see textile trades
Cobham, Lady Frances 54
common law 20
conciliation 101–2
conduct literature 21, 25, 30, 69, 72, 95, 111
contraception 69, 70
convents 38, 89, 90, 91
  see also nuns
Conway, Sir Edward 1, 4, 53, 64–5
Cooke, Ann 12, 16, 52
Cooke, Sir Anthony 12
Cooke, Elizabeth 12, 52
Cooke, Mildred 12, 52
Copley, Catherine 57
Copley, Dame Elizabeth 57
Coppin, Richard 87
Cornelius, Alice 40
courtesy literature 26
courts 21, 98–109 passim

church 20–1, 39, 65, 71, 81, 93
Coventry, Countess of 42
Cowper, William 3
Craven, Lady 56
Cromwell, Oliver 75
Crooke, Helkiah 3
Cyprian 36

dairying 77
Dakins, Margaret *see* Hoby, Lady
    Margaret
Dalton, Michael 98, 108
Daniel, Samuel 39, 53, 54
Davies, Lady Eleanor 43
defamation 21, 98, 99, 105–6, 107,
    109
Denton, William 14
Dering, Lady Unton 57
Descartes, René 45
divorce 27, 33, 52–3, 68, 83, 91, 96
Dod, John 25, 27
Donne, John 42, 54
double-standard 109
Dowland, John 54
dowries 1, 28, 52, 53, 64, 76, 89
Drake, Judith 33, 45
Dudley, Lord Robert *see* Leicester,
    Earl of

Edward IV (1461–83) 51
Elizabeth I (1558–1603) 2, 8,
    48–50, 53–4
  accession of 14, 47
  education of 12
Elizabeth of York 41
Elyot, Sir Thomas 43
emigration 74, 75
enclosures 56, 100–1, 111
  see also riots
English Civil Wars 2–3, 14, 18, 24,
    54–7, 111–2
  breakdown of censorship during
    18, 32, 96
  fatalities 74–5, 84, 112
  gaps in registration during 21,
    63, 75

Erasmus, Desiderius 11, 12, 40
Essex 21, 100, 102–3
Essex, Earl of 52–3, 83
estates literature 23
Eve 17, 32, 37, 43
  and Adam 3, 23,
Evelyn, John 39, 45, 98
Exeter 77, 88

Fanshawe, Lady Anne 19, 55, 71
Faversham 90
Fell, Margaret 33, 43, 96,
felony 92, 99–100, 102, 103, 104,
    107, 109
  see also bigamy, infanticide,
    witchcraft
feme covert 1, 74, 79
feme sole 74, 79
feminist theory vii, 4, 12, 14, 16–7,
    24, 33, 34, 112
Fisher, John 41
Fitzherbert, John 77
Flodden, battle of (1513) 51
Fontanus, Nicholas 60
Fox, George 97
Foxe, John 9, 92
Freind, Mrs 39
Frencham, Agnes 103
Frenchebourn, Ann 108
Frenchebourn, Thomas 108
funeral sermons 8–10, 29

Gataker, Thomas 25, 27
gender vii, 12, 13, 32, 34, 107
  crisis 78–9, 110
  construction 4, 24, 25, 27, 28,
    33, 87, 111
Gibson, Thomas 3
Gilbert, Adrian 53
Glandfield, Elizabeth 88
Gloucester, Richard Duke of *see*
    Richard III
godly lives 29
Gold, Mercy 70
golden legend 7

Goodman, Christopher 48, 49,
Gore, Joan 103
gossip 107, 111
Gosynhill, Edward 31
Gouge, Elizabeth (Calton) 28
Gouge, William 25, 28, 69
Gregory I, Pope 36
Grey, Lady Jane 12, 39, 50, 92,

Halkett, Lady Ann 19
Harley, Lady Brilliana 42, 53,
    57–8, 64–5, 69–70
  commonplace book of 95
  letters of 19, 66–7
Harley, Brilliana 1, 66
Harley, Dorothy 1
Harley, Edward 1, 70
Harley, Elizabeth 1
Harley, Margaret 1
Harley, Sir Robert 53, 64–5, 66
Harley, Robert 70
Harper, Joan 104
Hay, Lucy, Countess of Carlisle 55
Hays, Mary 9
Henrietta Maria 54–5
Henry VI (1422–61) 51
Henry VII (1485–1509) 51
Henry VIII (1509–47) 50, 51, 52,
    82, 86, 89, 91
Hereford 57
Herefordshire 19, 21, 42, 57–8, 64,
    66–7, 78
hermaphrodites 23
Heywood, Thomas 7
Hickes, George 45
Hit-him-home, Joan 17
Hoby, Lady Margaret 19, 39, 52,
    62, 94–5
homily on the state of matrimony
    (1563) 24–5, 30, 108
homosexuality 23
hospitals 81, 88, 89
Howard, Lady Frances 52–3, 83–4
Howard, Henry, Lord 50
Howard, Lady Jane 38

humanism 11, 12, 13, 26, 35, 36–7,
    42
Huntingdon, Countess of 39
husbands 1, 19–20, 24–5, 26, 37,
    56, 93, 112
  see also marriage, wives
Hutchinson, Lucy 19, 35, 64

idolatry 49
illegitimacy 61, 102–3,
industrial revolution 6, 9, 73
infanticide 70, 83, 92, 98, 102–3
inflation 74, 105
Inwood, Margery 93
Ireland 3, 74, 75

Jerome, St 23, 36
Jewring, Ann 102
Jezebel 49
Joceline, Elizabeth 28, 29, 43–4, 69
John, Dame Philippa 91
jointure 64
Julian of Norwich 90

Katherine of Aragon 36, 42, 51
Kempe, Margery 90
Kempis, Thomas à 41
Knox, John 14, 48–9, 58

lactation 69
Lambarde, William 99, 100
Langham, Lady Elizabeth 29
larceny 100
Latymer, William 42
Leicester, Robert Earl of 54
Leigh, Dorothy 29, 43
Leslie, John 50
levellers 55–7
Lewys, Joyce 92
Lincoln, Countess of see Clinton,
    Elizabeth
Line, Anne 94
Lisle, Lady Honor 66
literacy 18, 32, 35, 40, 41, 45–6,
    71, 79

Locke, Anne 95
Locke, John 5, 33, 46
lollards 41, 86, 87
London 40, 74, 76, 79, 81, 82, 83, 91, 95, 107
Lucretia 30
Lucy, Lady Alice 29
Luther, Martin 10

maisons dieu 88
Maisters, Widow 93
Makin, Bathsua 32, 33, 39, 44
Malebranche, Nicolas 45
Margaret, of Anjou 8, 51
Margaret, St of Antioch 88
marian martyrs 15, 56–7, 92, 94
Markham, Gervase 77
Marlborough, Duchess of *see* Churchill, Sarah
Marret, Jane 107
marriage 10, 11, 23, 24–7, 30, 33–4, 60–8, 74, 76–7
  alliances 52–3
  arranged 64, 67
  clerical 25, 27–8, 67–8
  negotiations 51, 64–5, 111
  and women's property rights 20
  remarriage 27, 65–6, 96
  see also breach of promise, husbands, wives
Marrow, Thomas 100
Mary I (1553–8) 2, 48–9, 53, 86, 92
  accession of 14, 47, 50
  education of 12, 42
Mary II (1688–94) 2, 44, 58
Mary of Modena 58
Mary, Queen of Scots 14, 47, 50, 54
Matilda, Empress 2
May games 32
medicine 3, 12, 19, 23, 60, 112
  humoral 3
men 1–2, 12, 23, 26, 30, 35, 37, 43, 46, 49, 77, 110–11
men-midwives 81, 82–3

menopause 104
menstruation 70
Messenger, Cecile 88
midwifery manuals 82
midwives 70, 76, 82–4, 87, 93, 111
Mildmay, Lady Grace 19, 67
Milton, John 27
miscarriage 70
Montague, Lady 56
More, Margaret 12, 16
More, Sir Thomas 12
Moswell, Katherine 68
Mulcaster, Richard 37
Munda, Constantia 17

Neville, Cicely, Duchess of York 41, 51
Neville, Henry 56
Newcastle, Duchess of *see* Cavendish, Margaret
Norfolk, Elizabeth Duchess of 51
Norwich 68, 81, 90, 91
nuns 88, 89–90, 91
  see also convents
nursing 81

original sin 111
Oxford 80, 84,

Packington, Dame Dorothy 57
parish registers 63
parliament 48, 55
  elections 1, 57
  long parliament 54–5
  petitions to 55–7
  statutes 48, 95, 98, 99–100, 102, 103, 104, 106, 107, 109
  see also voting
Parr, Katherine 39
Parry, Blanche 54
Paston family 64, 66
patriarchy 2, 4–5, 11, 27–8, 32, 49, 78–9, 87, 110, 112
patronage 14–15, 42, 47–8, 51, 52, 53, 59, 111

Paul, St 3, 12, 25, 26, 29, 67, 86
Pepper, Elizabeth 92
Pepys, Paulina 61
Pepys, Samuel 61
Perkins, William 28, 42
petty treason 98
plague 74, 81, 84, 89,
Plato 36
pleading the belly 83, 100
Plutarch 7
Pole, Anne 41
Pole, Margaret, Countess of
    Salisbury 51, 52
Ponet, John 48, 49
poor, the 11, 18, 68, 76, 84, 88, 95
poor relief 81, 105
population 74–5, 84, 89
    urban 76, 79
Pory, John 54
preaching, by women 87, 96
pregnancy 62, 68–9, 70, 83, 88, 108
    bridal 65
    see also pleading the belly
primogeniture 1
print culture 2, 34, 36, 79
    see also books
privy chamber 53, 54,
probate 19–20, 40–1,
property 19–20
prostitution 81–2
protestantism 2–3, 10, 11–12, 13,
    15, 21, 24, 25, 26–7, 48–9, 86,
    89, 92–3, 94, 104, 110
puritanism 10, 11–12, 21, 42, 53,
    61, 94–5

quakers 87, 96–7,
querelle des femmes 16–17, 30–1,
    34, 79

Ramesdale, Joan 68
rape 107–8
Ratcliffe, Mrs 95
reformation, The vii, 2, 3, 5, 10,
    11, 110, 111–12

Henrician 51–2, 88, 91
    religious disputes of 15, 47, 48
renaissance 5, 12, 13
resistance theory 49
rhetoric 36
Richard III (1483–85) 51
riots 56, 100–1
Rivers, Lady 55
Roos, Lord 27
Roper, Margaret see More,
    Margaret
Russell, Lady Elizabeth see Cooke,
    Elizabeth
Russell, Lady Rachel 58

Salisbury 76, 81
Salter, Thomas 37
Sarah 24
schools 36, 38, 39–40, 44, 89
scolding 13, 21, 30, 31, 78, 79, 106
Scot, Reginald 104–5
Scotland 3, 75
    witch trials in 105, 106
Scudamore, Lady Mary 54
sects 3, 96, 97
Selden, John 27
Seneca 36
servants 6, 27, 45, 61, 68, 73, 76, '
    77–8, 80, 90
sexual difference 1, 4, 112
Sharp, Jane 82
shopkeeping 79
Sidney, Mary (Dudley) 54
Sidney, Mary, Countess of
    Pembroke 16, 53
sieve and shears 103–4
signature, as evidence of literacy
    18, 36, 40
Smith, Abigail 65
Smith, Henry 25
Smith, Sir Thomas 48
Somerset, Edward Duke of 52, 64
Sowernam, Esther 17
Speght, Rachel 16–17,
Stafford, Lady Dorothy 54

Star Chamber 101
Starr, Mrs 71
Stonor family 66
Strickland, Agnes and Elizabeth 9
Stubbes, Katherine 29
Stubbes, Philip 29
Suffolk, Katherine, Duchess of 52, 64, 92
Suffolk, Mary, Duchess of 51
Surrey, Henry Earl of 38
Swetnam, Joseph 16, 31

Talbot, Elizabeth, Countess of Shrewsbury 62
The Taming of the Shrew 32
Tattle-well, Mary 17
Taylor, John 17, 31
Taylor, Thomas 25
Terling 76
textile trades 75–6, 77, 78, 79, 81
Thatcher, Margaret 2
theft 21, 99–100
Thornton, Alice 69, 71
Thynne, Lady Isabella 55, 56
Thynne, Joan 67
Thynne, Maria 67
Tonge 88
towns 76, 79–81, 88–9
Trapnel, Anna 43, 96
Tyler, Margaret 43

Vere, Lady Mary 53, 64–5, 66
Verney, Sir Ralph 14
Virgin Mary 11, 12, 32, 88, 91, 93
Vives, Juan Luis 11, 12, 36–7, 42, 43
Voragine, Jacobus de 7
voting 1–2, 24, 112

wages 10, 61, 73, 74, 76, 77–8, 84
Wales 3

Walker, Anthony 101–2
Ward, Margaret 94
Ward, Mary 91
Warham, William 91
Warwick 76
Warwick, Countess of 101–2
weaning 69–70
Wells, Mother 93
Wenham, Jane 106
wet-nursing 43, 69–70, 82
Whately, Martha (Hunt) 27
Whately, William 25–6, 27, 30
Whitney, Isabella 43
widows 20, 23, 45, 60, 80–1, 93, 107
wife-beating 30, 108, 109
William III (1688–1702)
wills 19–20, 40–1, 63, 87–8, 90, 94, 98
Wiltshire 13, 78, 107
witchcraft 14, 21, 92, 98, 102, 103–7
witches
   midwives as 83
   women as 13, 23, 78, 104–5, 106, 109
wives 23, 45, 46, 60, 73, 93, 107
   of clergy 28, 67–9
   of merchants 79
   obedience to husbands 17, 24, 29, 30, 33–4, 49, 95–6
   occupations of 76, 77, 79–80
   property of 20
   see also feme covert, husbands, marriage, wife-beating
Wood, Mary 70
Wood, Thomasine a 92
Woolley, Hannah 33
Xanthippe 30–1

York 81, 95, 107

HH LEARNING CENTRE
HARROW COLLEGE